*Ralph R. Teetor*

# ONE MAN'S VISION

## The Life of Automotive Pioneer
## Ralph R. Teetor

MARJORIE TEETOR MEYER

Guild Press of Indiana
Indianapolis

Guild Press of Indiana, Inc.
6000 Sunset Lane
Indianapolis, IN  46208




Library of Congress Number 95-77508




ISBN: 1-878208-66-7 (hardcover)
ISBN:1-878208-67-5 (paperback)




Manufactured in the United States of America.

## Dedication

To God belongs the glory . . .
Who still is working miracles in our lives.

# Contents

# Acknowledgments

Nowhere has our interdependence with other people been demonstrated more vividly to me than in the research and writing of this book. The contribution of memories, papers, pictures, advice, long distance calls, time, and encouragement from so many friends and relatives has been both heartwarming and humbling. First, I am indebted to my father and his secretaries, who filed copies of letters, clippings, pictures, and articles like packrats, resulting in a paper trail of personal and corporate history which has become the backbone of this narrative. My father preserved many of the early corporate records, and Bob Beeson provided a priceless file of Perfect Circle publications. *The Hagerstown Exponent* has recorded the weekly drama of most every event of note in the Hagerstown community since 1882. The materials were available. As I searched for an author, Nancy Kriplen, with professional wisdom, convinced me that I should write the story myself, and led me to editor Nancy Baxter who, with infinite patience, cheerful encouragement, and caring insight, pulled me far beyond what I thought was possible.

Information, stories, and pictures were contributed by many members of this still large, but now scattered, family: Jack Teetor, Dan's son; Dibbie Teetor, Don's wife, and Tom Teetor and Connie Rodie, their son and daughter; Debora Leadbetter and Christeen Anderson, Winnie's daughters; Ted Van Antwerp, Nellie's nephew; Chris Keagy, George's son; Josephine Davis and Mary Bond, also cousins; Marion Hartley Todd and Gordon Murray, Blair Hartley's daughter and nephew. Chuck Teetor, Lothair's son, has researched much of our common ancestral history and generously provided the genealogical table printed in the back of this book. If you find that keeping track of all the Teetor cousins is confusing, you are not alone. Most of our friends have trouble with that, and sometimes we get mixed up too.

Our family's friends and business associates have opened their hearts to this project, keeping me historically accurate by relating personal vignettes and experiences. Some who responded so generously to my many questions were Landrum Bolling, Gene Stohler, Bob Beeson, Lyle Cummins, Jim Cope, Luther Parsons, Roscoe Bell, Don Beeson, Dallas Lunsford, Karl Sharp, Bob Myers, Marvin Mahoney, Floyd Sanders, Keith Reed, Bob Bruns, Melvin Bennett, Jack Vanderford, Bob Morris, Don McCullough, and Chauncy and Doris McNelly. Also, Max Knight, Ralph Shelly, Nora Wilhide, Walter Seeley, Jane Lacey, Fredette House Cash, Richard Harrison, Jack and JoAnne Warmoth, and Ed and Pauline Best. Last but not least, Woody Ulrich, Harold Rowe, Tom Hasbrook, Myron Hunt, Earl Daggy, Ed McConnell, Jack Swoveland, Betty Ice, Pat Mayer at Treaty Line Girl Scout Council; Joe Gilbert and the Society of Automotive Engineers; Phil Seybold and the Hagerstown Museum; the Hagerstown Library, the Wayne County Historical Museum, the Indiana Historical Society, the Indianapolis Motor Speedway Museum archives, and the University of Pennsylvania archives.

I am grateful to those who read and corrected the entire manuscript: Lyle Cummins, Jack Teetor, Charles Teetor, Ralph Meyer, Mary Zeigler, Sue Ellen Childs, Lucy Meyer, and Ruth Purcell. Each contributed valuable suggestions which improved quality and accuracy.

In addition to the books and papers identifed in the text, I consulted various other historical informational resources. Some of those included:

*The Legend of Chris Craft.* Jeffrey L. Rodengen, Write Stuff Syndicate, 1988.

*Memoirs of Wayne County*, Vol. 2. Western Historical Assn., 1912.

*The Hagerstown Centennial, 1832–1932: A Souvenir History.* Robert Bryson, Hagerstown Centennial Committee, 1932.

*Indiana-Built Motor Vehicles.* Wallace S. Huffman, Indiana Historical Society, 1994.

"200 Years, A Bicentennial Illustrated History of the United States." *U.S. News and World Report*, 1976.

*Men, Money, and Motors.* Theodore MacManus and Norman Beasley, Harper & Brothers, 1929.

*American Heritage Pictorial Atlas of United States History.* American Heritage Publishing Co,, Inc., 1966.

*The Complete Encyclopedia of Motorcars,* 1885 to the Present, E.P. Dalton & Co., Inc., 1973.

Finally I am indebted to my husband, children, and grandchildren whom I have neglected for months but who have loyally encouraged me, supported me and helped whenever they were asked. You have blessed me with patience without measure.

# Introduction

On March 17, 1995, my father, Ralph R. Teetor, was inducted into the Central Indiana Business Hall of Fame. As I prepared for the third time in seven years to accept such an honor in his name I was again reminded how important heroes are in all our lives. Several friends who knew my father have insisted over the years that I write the account of how he lived beyond the handicap of blindness to become a leader in business and in automotive engineering, to invent many things and to live a happy, fulfilled life. Those friends should take credit for my finally completing this book.

As the story told itself through the many people who worked and played with Ralph and the letters and papers which they generated, the narrative grew beyond a biography of Ralph Teetor. It borrowed pieces from the history of bicycles and the birth and development of the automobile industry in an America on the edge of major industrial change.

The story had to include a big chunk of the history of the family business, which was such an integral part of my father's life. Just before his fifth birthday Ralph watched an idea, a dream, and five thousand dollars, mostly borrowed, launch a company that would grow to world leadership as Perfect Circle Corporation. It is doubtful one could start any business today on such a shoestring.

My father's interests spread well beyond the business world to almost everything about life. Education, politics, literature and music all captured his enthusiasm and full attention. Even with all he did, he always had time—time to listen, time to consider and think, and time to create and enjoy life. Thus I hope this book is at least partially a reflection of the times in which he lived.

A NOTE TO THE READER:

In striving for historcal accurracy I have chosen to spell Teetor (Teeter) whichever way it would have been spelled at that particular time. Prior to 1914 some of the family used "-er" and others used "-or" but after 1914 it was all "-or." If the reader finds this confusing, so did the family, which is why it was finally changed.

M.T.M.
July 1995

# The Course is Set

Ralph R. Teeter was born August 17, 1890, in Hagerstown, Indiana, a village of nearly one thousand people near the Ohio border. What a joy he must have been for a father and mother still grieving for their only daughter, four-year-old Eva, who had died just the September before. Kate Teeter announced to all the admiring uncles and aunts who were gathered that hot summer day that she would name her son Ralph. "Ah, but there is another Ralph Teeter in the family, Abe's little boy," her husband objected.

"Oh, that's all right," she replied. "That Ralph lives way over in Indianapolis, sixty miles from here. They will probably never even meet." Nevertheless she added the middle initial "R" to her son's name for clarification.

Indeed, Indianapolis seemed a world away from Hagerstown in 1890. Sixty miles was more than a full day's journey by horse and buggy—that is, if one owned such a luxury. The train, of course, shortened the trip to just over three hours, but it wasn't particularly easy; one had to pay the expensive fare to take one train to New Castle, then change to another train to ride the rest of the way. But within this young child's lifetime so much would change. The automobile would shrink that sixty miles to scarcely an hour, finally providing the mobility and freedom that brought Indiana villages from their provincial isolation to participation in the world. And the child born that day would play a remarkable role in the development of the automobile which caused such a revolution in American life.

Ralph's Teeter ancestors came from the village of Schwarzenau in what was then the principality of Wittgenstein, not far north of what is now Frankfurt, Germany. They were Dunkards, one of the groups of "plain people" who dressed without adornment and demanded that their members live by a Biblical moral code in the Anabaptist tradition. In future years this family would put aside its distinguishably drab garments and become members of the Brethren Church. Jorg Dieter arrived in Philadelphia in September, 1729, on the ship *Allen*, seventy days after it left Rotterdam. His son settled in Morrison Cove, near Cumberland County, Pennsylvania, in a Dunkard (or Pennsylvania Dutch) community just north of the present city of Altoona. For nearly a hundred years the family remained in that area, farming the rich land.

As was the case with the last names of many pioneer families, the name Teeter went through several metamorphoses. One version of these alterations was described in a letter from a Daniel Teeter to his niece in 1897. "Our name originally was Diederich, but that name was too long for the people, or at least some of them: '-ich' was left off and the name was shortened to Dieder, or Deeter, by which name we were always called in Pennsylvania when people were talking Dutch. Then when talking English the same people called us Teeter." Ralph Teeter's name would change once more before the spelling became final.

By 1823 the big Dunkard families had claimed the best of the land in the area around Morrison Cove, and many of the young sons, among them Ralph's great-grandfather Abraham Teeter, looked west. Word had come back that the fertile valleys in eastern Indiana offered good land and opportunity. So leaving his only horse at home, Abraham walked more than two hundred miles from Cumberland County to Wayne County, Indiana, to look over the frontier Hoosier state.

He must have liked what he saw, because he walked back to Pennsylvania to bring his wife, Elizabeth, their two small children, and all their possessions in a covered wagon to settle in Indiana. He chose a lovely piece of land near friends and relatives on the banks of Nettle Creek in Wayne County, built a house, cleared and planted, and fathered eight more children. Within a few years he was operating his own gristmill, grinding the grain from nearby farms.

Three of his children died while still very young, at least one of these in the cholera epidemic that swept through Indiana in the early 1830s. The other seven grew to adulthood and built their homes in a loose cluster around their father's mill in an area which became known as Teeter Town, two miles north of the present Hagerstown.

Abraham's mill was housed in a surprisingly large building constructed of sawn, not hewn, timbers and siding, probably prepared in the Stonebraker-Murray sawmill nearby. He rerouted the water from Nettle Creek through a race to a huge wooden waterwheel shafted to a series of large wooden gears which then turned a large grindstone, no small task in an age just beginning to demonstrate significant mechanical progress. Abe passed along to many of his descendants a distinct talent for mechanics and a fascination with almost any machine.

One day when an itinerant peddler came through Teeter Town showing his wares, a wonderful wall clock with a very loud tick caught the attention of Abe and his wife, Lizzie. Since up to that time no one in Teeter Town owned any kind of clock, pacing their days by their work and the sun, it is doubtful that they had felt the need to know what time it was. It had to be the mechanical precision that enchanted them. But in this barter-oriented frontier village, Abe had nothing near the twenty dollars needed for the wonderful time-telling machine. The savvy peddler suggested that he leave the clock with Abe and Lizzie until he returned the following year, at which time they could pay him the twenty dollars or return the clock to him. Of course they couldn't resist such a good offer. The clock was soon ticking on the parlor wall.

As the months went by, the family found they enjoyed knowing the time of day and possibly also the prestige accruing to the owner of such a fine machine. They did not want to part with the clock when the peddler returned, so the twenty dollars had to be earned. Abe and his oldest son, by now an adult, took their axes and walked the ninety miles or so to the Ohio River to chop down trees and cut firewood to sell to the passing riverboat captains. It took them a full month to earn the twenty dollars, and when they had finished, they walked back home. The peddler returned, the debt was paid, and the fascinating clock continued to tick on the parlor wall.

Abe and his sons also took part in the canal-building drama in eastern Indiana. In 1846 the Whitewater Canal was completed from Cincinnati to Cambridge City, Indiana, just eight miles south of Hagerstown, which by that time was becoming a thriving community. Surrounded by rich farmland, it included flour mills, a barrel factory, a tannery and pork-packing plant, an iron foundry, and several sawmills. Anticipating great commercial advantages from the construction of the canal, leading citizens formed a stock company to raise money to bring the canal the remaining eight miles to Hagerstown. The Dunkard religion did not permit its people to lend or invest money in the new stock company, so to contribute their share to this important endeavor the Dunkards, including Abe and his sons, brought their teams, scoops, and labor and worked alongside the hired hands to bring the canal to Hagerstown. The link was completed in 1847 and was contributing to the economic prosperity of the region when floods destroyed lower sections of the canal about 1865. By that time the railroads were coming through with cheaper, faster, and more dependable transportation, and the canal era was about to pass.

Zachariah, Ralph Teeter's grandfather, was born in 1836, one of Abe's younger sons. He learned the three "R's" and a bit of history in the traditional pioneer school using the famous *McGuffy Reader*. But his birthright was that of a master craftsman. Zachariah built a house near town, ran his father's mill, and became known for his skill and creativity in the fashioning of iron, stone, or wood tools and structures needed in the early settlements. He married Barbara Hoover, who bore him eight children—Ralph's father was the eldest. Since Zachariah was lovable and easygoing, but a poor businessman, Barbara ran the business side of the mill. After she died suddenly at age forty-eight, Zach and his younger children went through some trying years.

Meanwhile, across the Atlantic, Ralph's maternal grandfather was preparing to come to the new land. Johann Rauh was also a Dunkard, living in what is now Bavaria, Germany. In 1838 he finished his apprenticeship as a cooper, married Caroline Facialt, and began traveling about the country making barrels. The government required each man to carry a small book with him which would serve as a kind of passport. In addition to the places to which he ventured, the book included the rules under which each Bavarian craftsman must live, rules which specifically prohibited him from leaving the country under penalty of a severe fine. After working three years in Germany, Johann sailed for America with his wife and two children. Nothing more was ever recorded in his book except the birth of his children.

It must have taken considerable courage to leave behind family, friends and language to endure the hardships of a long ocean voyage to a strange new world. On these ships families were expected to provide their own food for the voyage. If they ran out of food, it had to be purchased from the captain, who charged a dear price. Johann related that when they arrived at the mouth of the Chesapeake Bay, it was evening. The captain anchored, wishing to wait for daylight to navigate the long, treacherous waterway leading into Baltimore. The passengers celebrated their arrival in the new world with a big party on the ship, eating all their remaining food—they expected to be on land early the next day. Later that night a storm blew the immigrants back out to sea. It took nearly two more weeks to sail back to Baltimore, and everyone had to buy food from the captain. So after seven weeks at sea, Johann arrived in Baltimore with only fifty cents, his guitar and his own ingenuity.

First the family found a room where Caroline and the children could stay. Then Johann stood on the street, playing his guitar for the money to buy food and pay the rent. He soon found work as a cooper, and they settled into Baltimore life, eventually producing six more children.

Exactly five years after arriving in the New World, the Rauhs became United States citizens, and Johann changed his name to John Rowe to sound more properly American. In 1855 Caroline and her youngest child died. Left with seven small children, Johann rather quickly married Lydia Brown. Lydia's father had already migrated to the fertile valleys of Hagerstown, Indiana, so three years and two more children later the Rowe family joined him, moving to Hagerstown too. Here they built a house and had nine more children. The second of Lydia and Johann's children, Kate Colombia Rowe, and the eldest son of Zachariah, John Hamilton Teeter, were married August 25, 1881. When these pioneer families joined, they brought to the union the strong moral code of the German Baptist Church (Dunkard), a tradition of hard work and self-reliance, and an innate and creative mechanical talent that would soon carry them into a full realization of the American dream.

John, who was Ralph's father, was born two miles north of Hagerstown on November 8, 1860. He went to the local one-room school for several years, attaining about a fifth-grade education. One of his classmates was his future wife, Kate. The two lived only a couple of miles apart and played together as children. One can easily imagine how this young couple, each of them from a large family, would find that they had much in common. John lived at home and worked at the mill his grandfather had built until, when he was twenty-one, he took a job with the Deering Binder Company in Nashville, Tennessee. Although he married Kate just before he left for Nashville, it appears that she remained in Hagerstown. A year later he came home in the poor health which was to plague him for the rest of his life. Some people said John's illness was a result of the hot, humid climate in Nashville; others surmised the condition was Parkinson's disease or diabetes. No one ever knew what the problem was, and the family flatly denied all guesses. Whatever it was, it was not fatal, for he lived another fifty-seven years. He was described as a gentle, quiet man, interested in others, with a quick, sometimes rowdy, sense of humor.

On his return to Hagerstown, utilizing his experience in sales, John became a clerk in the insurance office of Colonel John Hartley, where he sold fire insurance and learned business and administrative skills which would become invaluable in future years. On the side he ran a bicycle building and repair business with one of his brothers and a cousin. His father's family was going through hard times after Barbara's death, and money was scarce for them all.


Kate Rowe had been born in Maryland and was a very young child when her family moved to Hagerstown. She was near the middle of her father's eighteen children, and she found much to do and many companions to do it with. Family life largely revolved around the long wooden kitchen table and benches which seated twenty-four, built by her father. She always described a happy childhood in a loving family, but when her turn came she reared an only child.

John and Kate Teeter began housekeeping in Hagerstown. In due time a daughter, Eva, was born, but she died of diphtheria just before her fourth birthday. Eleven months later their hopes for a family revived with the birth of Ralph. The editor of *The Hagerstown Exponent*, the weekly newspaper of the town, was so engrossed in reporting the preparations for the big Hagerstown fair that he was a week late announcing Ralph's birth. Finally he wrote, "A child was born to John Teeter." That was all. The Teeters were numerous, but obviously not the social leaders of the town.


With a population of nearly one thousand in 1890, Hagerstown was one of many small Midwestern villages poised on the edge of the Age of Progress. Its businesses, mills, slaughter and packing houses, and general stores served an agricultural constituency. The streets were not yet paved, but natural gas had been discovered nearby three years before, and gas streetlights were being installed. In his early childhood, Ralph spent many happy hours accompanying the lamplighter on his evening rounds. The Big Four Railroad had laid track on the towpath of the short-lived Whitewater Canal to Cincinnati, and the railroad's opening widened the market for the prosperous farms and mills. In winter, ice was cut into blocks from a small lake near town and stored in a large ice house for use all through the summer. Nine years would pass after Ralph's birth before telephones were installed in Hagerstown, and eighteen years until electricity was available in Hagerstown homes.

Bicycles were immensely popular. Although two-wheeled, man-powered vehicles had been built early in the nineteenth century, the "high-wheeler" with pedals attached to the front axle was invented in France in 1861. Enthusiasm for this new "velocipede" rapidly spread across the United States. With the invention of the chain drive by

Harry Lawson in 1879, bicycles became safer and easier to ride. After that, each year brought new models of bicycles with ever more desirable improvements to the wonderful "wheels" which gave men easy access to quick travel, and women a freedom they had not dreamed of. This fairly simple machine appealed to the mechanical talents of the Teeter "boys," and all of them spent hours tinkering with these fascinating contraptions and making the repairs they often needed.

Money remained in short supply for the John Teeter family, and the panic of 1893 just prolonged the struggle. A letter from Ralph's father to his cousin Abe (the clock owner's grandson) in Indianapolis indicates the difficulties of making ends meet in the bicycle shop that they jointly managed:

*Hagerstown, Indiana 7/17/1894*

*Dear Cousin Abe: . . . We will send Browder's wheels [bicycle] to him today. If you will go down and set them up some evening for him before he comes home I will be under obligations to you. You know a lawyer don't know much and he might get the handle on the wrong end and not get the pedals on at all and say the wheel was no good. I would like for you to state to him whether or not the wheels are as good as could be built out of the material that was furnished us . . . I suppose you remember what Browder's wheels were to be, $86.00. Now Abe I will mention a little matter that you can use your good judgment in the matter. You know we were to build Browder's wheels for so much money just for the naked wheels and there was nothing said about pants, shirt, collar, or even a pair of suspenders. Now do you think it proper to charge for crating? If you do you can make the charge what you think right. It took me the best part of a day to do the work as I had to make one of the crates or nearly so. Well Abe I can't think of another darned thing to say and will close by promising to write more some other time.*

*Yours truly.*
*J. H. Teeter*

Fortunately it didn't take a lot of sophistication to be a businessman in Hagerstown, Indiana, in the 1890s.

John had four younger brothers and three sisters, all of whom lived most of their lives in Hagerstown. His son Ralph loved to spend time with his aunts and uncles, but only one of them, Charles, was to play a major part in Ralph's future.

Charlie Teeter was just fourteen when his mother Barbara died. Her death ended Charlie's one-room schoolhouse days, and he was indentured to a nearby farmer for three years. He remembered this time as the most miserable in his life, filled with hunger, cold, and backbreaking work. Still, he learned about the time's primitive farm equipment, and he began to think about how it could be improved. He vowed that some day he would be successful enough that he would never go hungry again.

After three years of work on the farm, Charlie obtained a scholarship to a Dunkard college in Lebanon, Ohio, which offered a one-year program for training teachers for one-room schools. He returned to his home school and taught there two years. Because school lasted only a few months in the winter when the children could be spared from the farm, teaching was never a full-time job. Charlie needed to work as a carpenter for the remaining months of the year. He had learned fine craftsmanship from his father and uncles and was by this time well prepared for the next step in his life.

By the early 1890s the bicycle enthusiasm which had swept Indiana had provided employment for most of the Teeter men in various shops in Indianapolis, Connersville, Shelbyville, and Hagerstown. Ralph's father and his cousin Abe, as we have seen, were busy making and repairing bicycles in their own shop. Charlie joined them for a while, learning every detail of bicycle manufacturing, but was working at a shop in New Castle when, in 1894, he built a fine bicycle for his young bride, Leora. No description of that bicycle has survived, but it was undoubtedly one of the new "safety" bicycles invented fifteen years before with a chain connecting the pedals to the back wheel. We can also be sure that the workmanship was superb. Leora's cousin Charles Hartley, whose father was John Teeter's insurance boss, visited her and admired her new bicycle. Hartley also worked for the Chicago and Northwestern Railroad. What happened after that is best told in Ralph Teeter's own words:

*Charles Hartley asked, "Can there be some device made that can be attached to a bicycle so that the bicycle can be ridden on a railroad track?" He explained that there were many occasions on which they would send a man out into the country from the towns and cities to inspect the railroad bridges, et cetera, but they had no way to transport the inspector except to operate the locomotive. He knew that it would be of great service to them if a machine such as a bicycle could be ridden by the inspector, a machine light enough that the inspector could lift it from the track to permit the passing of trains.*

*Charlie drew the first rough designs for a railway cycle on the floor of his small shop and, after considerable work, came up with a design which filled all requirements. His employer, Mr. Shupp, encouraged him to build an experimental machine and allowed him to use the machinery in his shop to build the car on his own time. This was done at night and on Sundays after working six ten-hour days each week. The car he built in the New Castle bicycle repair shop he rode successfully on the Pennsylvania Railroad from New Castle to Hagerstown where his brother, John Teeter (my father) and I were waiting to greet him. This is one of the vivid memories I still have even though I was not yet five years old. It was December of 1894. . . .*

*After Charlie Teeter built the experimental cycle car it was decided that, if sufficient capital could be raised, they would organize a company to manufacture and market the cars. Charles Hartley was so certain that railroads would buy the cars that he invested twenty-five hundred dollars in the venture. The members of the Teeter family were able to borrow a few hundred dollars each which, with some work pledges, brought the total capitalization to five thousand dollars. The Railway Cycle Manufacturing Company incorporated February 16, 1895.*

*Although I was a very small boy, I can remember when Uncle Charlie and my father rented from William Stonebraker about thirty feet of the north end of his old warehouse . . . They also made arrangements to buy power provided by an old steam engine which had operated some machinery in the building. They purchased three or four secondhand machines which made up the company's complete machine capacity for the first few years.*

Thus, a major industrial corporation was born. It quickly developed a national then an international market for their much-needed product. Seven months after incorporating, the Railway Cycle Manufacturing Company shipped two cycle cars to Russia and had orders for three more. Within two years orders were coming from Europe, South America, Africa, Australia, and all parts of the United States.

Charles Teeter also wrote about that first year:

*At the close of 1895 the company had about fifteen hundred dollars to show for the five thousand dollars paid in. It was then reincorporated for ten thousand dollars and we succeeded in selling seven hundred dollars additional stock, but our friends had no confidence in our enterprise and consequently the first five thousand dollars and the additional seven hundred dollars was all the actual cash ever put into that company or its succeeding companies. . . .*

*In 1900 the name of the company was changed to Light Inspection Car Company.*

By 1900 many of the inspection cars were now powered by engines rather than the cycle mechanism. Charles had worked for four years, discarding a dozen failures, to develop a single-cylinder gasoline engine which could propel the little car.

From the earliest time he could remember (which was exceptionally young) Ralph Teeter's favorite pastime was to be with the men at the "shop," first fixing bicycles, then after the new company began, making cycle cars. To him this was much more fun than playing children's games. His patient uncles taught him to play-work alongside them at a very early age. He also loved to accompany his father in the horse and buggy on frequent trips into the country to meet insurance customers and examine claims. So important were those trips to Ralph that he would sit very quietly during the meetings so that he would continue to be allowed to go along.

Ralph Teeter's most vivid early memories, however, were of the Columbian Exposition, the great Chicago World's Fair of 1893 commemorating Columbus' discovery of America four hundred years before. The Pennsylvania Railroad ran a special "Fair Excursion Train" from Cincinnati to Chicago right through Hagerstown for six dollars and fifty cents round-trip. Ralph and his father rode the train, eager to take in the showcase of industrial progress. They marveled at the huge Allis engine and the dynamo, so important to their future, but now only a curiosity to them. They examined George Westinghouse's alternating-current generator and a Singer sewing machine—treadle, of course. The sole horseless carriage on display did not attract a great deal of attention. Ralph, a few weeks short of three years old, was most thrilled by Mr. Ferris' wonderful wheel, 264 feet high, that would sweep him and his father up over the crowds so he could see farther than he had ever seen. At night the panorama spread out below the first Ferris Wheel was a dazzling display of many-hued electric lights playing on fountains and pavilions. This first extavaganza of American electricity created a fairyland of glittering beauty that became one of the most popular attractions of the fair. Although he was only three years old, Ralph remembered it for the rest of his life.

Ralph's early childhood was developing in a normal, happy way. Then an accident occurred that was to change this gifted boy's life forever. It was an event that, as a grown man, he preferred never to discuss; in fact, he managed to live his life almost as if it had never happened. The most detailed account comes, then, not from people who knew him, but from the local newspaper of the time, *The Hagerstown Exponent*. The same editor who had scarcely managed a birth announcement had been won over by this little five-year-old boy who suddenly found himself involved in a tragic struggle:

*March 25, 1896: John Teeter's little boy met with a serious accident Friday last. While playing with a knife he in some way thrust the blade into one of his eyes cutting the ball badly, and may lose the sight. The best surgical talent was employed to dress the wound.*

*May 13, 1896: Ralph Teeter is having a serious time with his eyes for ten days past. The sight of the wounded eye is entirely gone but the wound has healed and left no marks. But the other eye has been inflamed and Ralph has been confined to a dark room for ten days or more.*

*May 20, 1896: Little Ralph Teeter is having a serious time lately with his wounded eye. His doctor thought it best to remove the ball of the afflicted eye and he was taken to Indianapolis last Thursday and the operation was performed. His other eye is reported as some better today. His parents are both with him.*

*June 10, 1896: Little Ralph Teeter is at home again and can see partially with one eye and has prospects of the eyesight improving. He is in good health which is much in his favor. He is perfect in form, a very bright little fellow, and many hearts have ached in sympathy for him and his sad misfortune.*

*October 7, 1896: Little Ralph Teeter is again threatened with total blindness. His parents have just returned from Cincinnati with him where he was examined and they were informed that a most critical operation was necessary to even have him retain what little sight he now has, and even this result was doubtful. They will return with him tomorrow and the most skilled talent that can be had will perform the operation.*

*October 21, 1896: The Railway Cycle Company received yesterday, by express, a very fine southern mocking bird as a present from J. H. Brothers, of Meridian, Wisconsin. Mr. Brothers is a railroad official who bought one of the Company's light inspection cars a short time ago, and being so well pleased with it he sends the bird to them in assurance of his appreciation of the machine. The bird was turned over to little Ralph Teeter who has been so unfortunate with his eyes.*

*November 18, 1896: John Teeter took his son, Ralph, to Cincinnati Monday to have his eye treated. Another operation will be necessary soon as there has been no improvement.*

*January 20, 1897: Little Ralph Teeter, of whom until lately it was thought by his physicians that in all probability, unless a critical operation would be performed, he would lose his eyesight, has in the past week or two showed decided symptoms of a total recovery of the sight of his eye, the sight of one being entirely destroyed some time since in the accidental stabbing while using a knife of that member.*

*June 2, 1897: The ladies of the Christian aid society met on Monday night at the home of Mrs. John H. Teeter. Master Ralph Teeter had just received an immense basket of magnolias and jessamine, both buds and full-blown flowers, from a friend in the state of Mississippi. The ladies were enthusiastic in their praise of the lovely flowers, which were indeed beautiful and of interest profound.*

During the autumn of 1897, John and Kate made several trips to Chicago, becoming acquainted with Judge William G. and Ruth Ewing, Christian Science practitioners who lived there.

The final entry in *The Exponent* follows:

*December 8, 1897: Mrs. John Teeter has returned after a two week stay, from Chicago, where she went with her little son, Ralph, that he might receive treatment from a Christian Scientist of that place. As is known, Ralph has been suffering for about a year with an injured eye, which for some time past has shown no improvement but rather a tendency to greater weakness. It is thought that the eye has been benefited by the treatment. That member seems to be in more healthy condition and the sight perceptibly stronger. Since their return he receives each day what is termed absent treatment through this Christian Scientist.*

However, physical healing did not progress. The condition is called *sympathetic opthalmia*, a condition in which a severe injury to one eye produces antibodies that attack the uninjured eye. At the time the cause was not known, its occurrence rare and unpredictable, but the only known prevention was immediate removal of the injured eye. In Ralph's case this was not performed quickly enough. His vision slowly faded, and by a year later it was entirely gone. It was a bitter disappointment. They had lost the battle, but this strong pioneer family still had more than enough courage and endurance to carry on the war.

A Teeter family portrait shows Joe, Charles, John, Frank, Zachariah, and Henry.
(Courtesy of Charles' grandson, Charles Teetor)

Charles Teetor's original workshop. Charles drew the first plans for the Railway
Inspection Car on the dirt floor.

*Abraham and Elizabeth Teeter, circa 1881.*

*Zachariah and Barbara Teeter, before 1884.*

*Charles and Joe Teeter with their high-wheel bicycles. The children are Neva Deardorff and Ralph Teeter, 1891.*

*John and Ralph Teeter on a "safety" bike, so called because it had equal-size wheels and a chain from the pedals to the rear axle, 1893.*

*Kate and John Teeter, Ralph's parents, circa 1895.*

*Charles Teeter worked four years to develop a small, powerful engine for the inspection car, 1900.*

*Ralph Teeter at about age four, 1894.*

*The original Railway Inspection Car was sold over the world to transport repairmen to keep the track clear. Here it is being ridden by John Teeter, 1895.*

4

1905—March 2, Car #0000 W M Ritten Lbr Co. D, 3' 6" 8425 ___ Repaired

| Date Shipped. | No. | Purchaser | Kind, | Gauge. | Gear | Odr |
|---|---|---|---|---|---|---|
| 1895 | | | | | | |
| May 15 | 1 | J P Tucker. Wiscasset, Maine. | D | 2' 0" | 6x20 | |
| June 17 | 2 | W D Draper. Chicago, Ill. | " | 4' 8½" Brake | " | |
| May 21 | 3 | C W Henry. R.M. Cedar Rapids, Iowa. | " | " | " | |
| 22 | 4 | J G Kendall R.M. Nogales, Ariz. | " | " | " | |
| 25 | 5 | F.H. Fechtig. P.A. Wilmington, N.C. | " | " | " | |
| 28 | 6 | H.A. Whiting, Wilmington Newborn & Norfolk Ry. | " | 4' 9" | | |
| 30 | 7 | W H Hinkle, M.S. Galveston Texas. | " | 4' 8½ | | |
| June 3 | 8 | S.R. Stubbs, Supn. Millville, N.J. | " | " | Brake | |
| 28 | 9 | C.H. Walton, Supt. Logansport Ind. on trial | " | " | on trial | |
| July 5 | 10 | W H Barrett, Train Master, Elmira N.Y. | " | " | | |
| Jan 10 | 10A | Walter F Aldrich. S. Blackstone Mass. | " | " | 7x25 | 17 |
| July 2, 1895 | 11 | Wisconsin Central Ry. Ashland, Wis. | D" | " | | |
| June 26 | 12 | Eastern Ry of Minn. West Superior, Wis. | " | " | | |
| 25 | 13 | E Pennington Supt. Minneapolis, Minn. | " | " | on trial | |
| 26 | 14 | Illinois Central R.R. Memphis Tenn. | " | " | | |
| July 11 | 15 | Michael Butler, Lineman, Missoula Mont. | " | " | | |
| June 28 | 16 | Thos Baily. Bay Mills, Mich. | " | " | | |
| 22 | 17 | Chester & Lenoir R.R. Per L.S. Nichols Supt. | " | 3. 0" | Brake | |
| July 13 | 18 | W.D. Draper Chicago Ill. | " | 4' 8½" Brake | | |
| 3, | 19 | M R Bongano, Ass't Mgr. Bou. Jersey R.R. | " | " | | |
| June 28 | 20 | Southern Ry Co. M & O Ry. | " | 4' 9" | | |
| July 15 | 21 | L R Gordon, Gen. Supt. Maravatio, Mex. | " | 3' 0" | | |
| " " | 22 | Western New & Penna Ry. Brocton N.Y. | D | 4' 8½ | | |
| Aug 28 | 23 | E.B. Denechaud, Mission Jct. B.C. | D | " | | |
| July 17 | 24 | W M Brown, Agt. C.M. & St P Ry. Iowa | " | " | | |
| 19 | 25 | Southern Pac. Co. San Francisco | " | " | on trial | |
| 20 | 26 | Sherman Shreveport & Southern Ry | " | " | | |
| 22 | 27 | San Francisco & North Pac. Ry. | " | " | | |
| 24 | 28 | Thos Owens Supt. D & S R R R | " | " | | |
| 26 | 29 | H P Wyman Pres't E R R Ry. for Dr Hodges | " | " | | |
| 27 | 30 | W B Lee Supt. Ridgeway Colo. | " | 3' 0" | | |
| Aug 1 | 31 | H.M. Barry Com. Merchant. Philadelphia for export to Russia | " | 5' 0" | | |
| 3 | 32 | A Billhardt, for export to Russia | " | " | | |
| 1 | 33 | Maine Central Ry. Waterville Me. | D | 4' 8½ | | |
| 3 | 34 | A Billhardt, for export to Russia | D | 5' 0" | | |
| 5 | 35 | G F Jones. M.D. Webbwood. Ont. | " | 4' 8½ on trial | | |
| 3 | 36 | P P & H L, R R Pittsburg | " | 4' 9" | | |
| 12 | 37 | Boston & Maine R R. | " | 4' 8½ | | |

*Railway Inspection Car shipping book, page 1, 1895. This log was kept for twelve years.*

*Ten men and a boy, Ralph, demonstrate the strength of the Railway Inspection Car, 1895. Just after this picture was taken this group rode the car eleven miles from New Castle to Hagerstown. At twilight they encountered a skunk on the track in front of them. The suit Ralph is wearing may still be buried in the backyard of his home.*

# Bicycles to Automobiles

By the time Ralph had finished the unsuccessful treatments for his eyes and the family had resigned themselves to the fact that he was not going to get better, Ralph was seven years old. His sight was nearly gone, and he had not been to school. What could he learn? *How* could he learn? Could he ever be independent, support himself, perhaps contribute to society? John and Kate must have pondered these questions. What could they do to help him? There were no services to aid the blind in Hagerstown. Nor was there much precedent for anyone without sight to accomplish a great deal, especially without an education. They hoped for a miraculous healing, but as each day passed and the healing didn't occur, they needed to deal with the practical necessities.

The Ewings, with whom they had consulted in Chicago, had a daughter who was organizing a private Christian Science school near her parents' home. It was decided that Ralph would spend the next few months there, learning as much as he could in first grade and studying Christian Science. Not much is known about this episode. Later in his life Ralph's only comments about it were that he was homesick and miserable in Chicago. In the fall of 1898 he enrolled in the public school in Hagerstown.

Education in Indiana had improved considerably since his father, mother, uncles, and aunts had attended the one-room schoolhouse in the country. A square two-story stucco building, containing eight classrooms and a small office, had been built near the center of town. The first eight grades met in the four rooms on the first floor, two grades and one teacher in each room. The second floor contained the high school. The only scheduled vacations were Thanksgiving and the week between Christmas and New Year's Day. School was out for the summer by mid-April, because the boys were needed to help with the planting on the farms. In Ralph's case the summer vacation provided four and a half wonderful months to spend without interruption in the mechanical work-play which had come to be the center of his life.

Ralph's grades were excellent. His mother read his lessons to him and drilled him on what he needed to remember, and his teachers tested him orally. He was reasonably popular with his peers, although he did not spend a great deal of time playing with them. He later told stories of exchanging presents with other children at birthday parties and participating in his share of mischievous pranks, such as dipping the braids of the girl sitting in front of him into his inkwell. But mostly he preferred to be with his uncles at the factory, observing them in his own way and learning how to use their tools and machines.

He walked all about the little town by himself, sensing where he was by hearing the echo of his footsteps change at the corner of a building, or by touching a familiar bush, or just counting the steps it took to walk from one landmark to another. Sometimes he would slide his shoe on the pavement or snap his fingers to give his ears a few more of the echoes which served as audible guidance to a doorway or telephone pole. He insisted anyone might hear those echoes as well as he could with a little practice. He could certainly hear the horses and buggies crunching down the unpaved streets. The early automobiles were even noisier than the horses and thus easy to locate by their sounds, enabling him to stay out of the way. Not until the late 1940s did the combination of paved streets and much quieter automobiles require him to give up his solo sauntering around town.

In adjusting to Ralph's gradual loss of sight, it appears that the family developed a remarkable philosophy. Essentially they lived their lives as if Ralph could see normally. The problem was never mentioned unless circumstances made it absolutely necessary. Certain accommodations were made, but the reasons for these alterations were never discussed. For example, Ralph's clothes were always put away in the same place in his closet or dresser, the brown socks in one corner, the black ones in another. The food on his plate was cut into bites before it was placed in front of him, and someone would casually mention what was there if Ralph didn't already know. Doors were either always closed or always open, *never* partly ajar; otherwise Ralph might run into the edge. If circumstances required a special request for help, that request was presented as an ordinary question. "What color is this tie?" or "Do you see any change in the temperature gauge?" Ralph commonly used expressions such as "Let me see it," or "I think I see the problem." The challenge which Ralph accepted was to live as completely normal a life as possible and accomplish whatever goals he chose to pursue.

Christian Science, which was at the turn of the century still a new religion, must be given a great deal of credit for the strength and reassurance it provided the family. The Christian Science interpretation of the Bible denies the reality of sin, disease, and death because they are not believed to be part of God's creation. The Bible states that God is the only creator and all He created was good, so handicaps do not really exist, at least in the spiritual and eternal world. Further, Christian Science emphasizes that prayer can overcome problems, and that God provides believers directly with the power to deal with whatever is necessary. It was a philosophy that reinforced Ralph's self reliance while encouraging and strengthening his hope for the future. Charles and Leora, then other family members and some neighbors, joined the little group of Christian Scientists who met together in Hagerstown, validating the beliefs of Ralph and his parents. At first they met in John and Kate's home for worship; later, they built a church in Hagerstown.

Ralph's secular life was also helping him develop tools to serve him well in the future. He loved to hear books read to him. Since he couldn't learn to read, there was no need to wade through the mindless beginning-reader stories which a child such as Ralph might find boring. In these very formative years his mother read to him over and over again until he knew them by heart books of the lives of men who would become his heroes: stories of DeWitt Clinton and his steamboat, Eli Whitney and the cotton gin, Benjamin Franklin, and Ralph's favorite—Thomas Edison. He could identify with their fascination with machinery, their striving to invent something better, and their thrill to push beyond the frontiers of knowledge.

After all, that was what was happening down at the factory. Charlie and the folks with whom he worked were continuously improving each new model of the cycle car, designing it to carry one man, then two, and finally improving it to operate without pedaling. Charlie was breaking new ground every day, laboring to invent a small, lightweight engine that would propel the cycle car. Since no powering device like that had ever been produced, he worked four years, building and rejecting a dozen engines, before he finally developed one that was small, yet powerful enough. Nor were the Teeters' ideas limited to engines. Patents were inexpensive and simple to obtain. Charlie and Zachariah were both collecting patents on such inventions as a robber-proof lock for freight trains and a device to straighten steel tubing. Whenever there was a need for a tool or piece of machinery which they didn't have, they made it if they could. They patiently discussed all of their ideas and methods with the bright little boy who was so eager to be a part of their mechanical world.

Ralph progressed from learning how to use hand tools to running all the machines, lathes, milling machines, grinders, and drills at the factory. The uncles taught him how to plan, measure, create, and polish to make something perfect in wood or metal. As his weak sight faded permanently, his senses of touch, hearing, and smell sharpened, and he learned to use and trust those senses. In a day when there was very little safety protection attached to machinery, serious accidents caused by misplaced fingers or caught-up clothing were not unusual even for careful workmen. Workers marveled at the skill Ralph developed in operating all these machines without serious injury.

By the time Ralph was ten he had become so skillful that his father built a shed onto the back of their house. In it he installed machines and tools to create a workshop for his son. After that, Ralph began spending most of his spare time working in his home shop although he never stopped dropping by the factory nearly every day to check on the progress there.

Later Ralph remembered a childhood almost free of parental discipline. Typical was the day that he threw a tantrum when his mother called him from his workshop to practice the piano. That ended the piano lessons. He bragged that as a young child he knew exactly where to fall as he ran to his room so that he could slide under the bed to escape his mother's switch. He stayed there until she gave up calling him to come out. Was he spoiled? Not in the sense that his character was made soft and selfish, certainly. Several of his cousins believed him to have been indulged and catered to because of his blindness. Without a doubt, that was true. But his stubbornness and determination to have his own way were necessary for his survival. He was going to need iron-willed perseverance to meet the adversity life had handed him. Now he needed to establish his identity in a world that was reluctant to allow him to be independent.

It was 1900, a perfect time and place for a boy of mechanical talent to be growing up. The automobile was in the process of being born. Inventors had been trying since the seventeenth century to add power to wheeled vehicles. Suddenly, during the decade of the 1890s, years of experimentation with engines, gears, fuels, and ignitions came together, enabling automotive pioneers to "get it right." In 1891 the first gasoline powered cars as we know them were created independently by Charles Black in Indianapolis and John Lambert in Anderson, Indiana. The Duryea brothers of Peoria, Illinois, and Elwood Haynes in Kokomo began building cars in 1894. By the end of the century Stanley, Winton, Olds, and others joined the parade. It was a time of intense industrial creativity, spurred on by the gospel of the American Dream according to Horatio Alger. But no other invention implied the heady romance, the prestige and the ability to alter the culture that the automobile promised for America.

By spring of 1902 there were a number of automobiles in use in Indiana, but Dr. Canaday owned the only car in Hagerstown, an Oldsmobile. It was described as "guided with a steering lever, with a horn alarm sounded by a rubber bulb. Oil lamp headlights. Solid rubber tires. No doors or top." That same spring Ralph, nearly twelve, decided to build a car himself, using Dr. Canaday's wonderful new Oldsmobile as a pattern.

Ralph's second cousin Dan, who lived in Indianapolis, came to Hagerstown to visit relatives that summer. Although Dan was four years older than Ralph, they were great friends; both enjoyed working on mechanical projects. When Dan arrived, he enthusiastically joined the car-building project. By this time Charlie had developed a fairly practical gasoline engine for the cycle car and the motorized version was being successfully sold all over the world. In fact, by 1902 his company was manufacturing engines which pumped well water and ran pneumatic hammers to chisel gravestones. It was not difficult for the boys to find a small engine which had been cast into some remote corner of the factory and secure permission to use it.

With that rejected engine Ralph and Dan began to build the car. Working on it all summer, machining each part by hand, they completed the car in late August. In a town as small as Hagerstown nothing of even slight consequence went unnoticed, and the project caught the eye of a local young man, Cash Ginther, who was an aspiring newspaper reporter.

He wrote about the boys' little car and sold the story to *The Cincinnati Enquirer*. The article was first printed November 9, 1902, and was copied in several other Midwestern newspapers. Then *The New York Herald* sent a reporter to Hagerstown to interview Ralph and to photograph him in the car and in his workshop, publishing the human-interest story on December 21, 1902.

All this attention in print contained heady praise for a boy twelve years old. But there was one remarkable omission. Neither the original article nor *The New York Herald* story said one word about Ralph Teeter's not being able to see. With all the flowery admiration, one would expect that fact would have been included. Did the reporters not notice? Cash would have been aware of Ralph's blindness because he lived in Hagerstown. Perhaps Ralph's father asked him not to mention it. It is possible, though, that the New York reporter never realized that Ralph was blind. The omission was to be a characteristic pattern. Throughout his life Ralph thoroughly enjoyed the frequent opportunities to meet people who either did not realize or did not believe that he could not see. Never would he tell them. Functioning so well that he could "pass" for sighted seems to have been another part of his lens on reality in a dark world.

# A STORY OF SUCCESS

RALPH TEETER.

RALPH TEETER, the twelve-year-old son of Mr. and Mrs. John H. Teeter, of Hagerstown, Ind., is probably the youngest practical electrician in that state. He not only has a thorough understanding of the theory of the subject of electricity, but is able to apply his knowledge in dozens of ways.

Ralph is permitted to pursue his investigations in his own way. His home contains many instruments in which electricity in some form or other is applied. These instruments range from electric call bells to the best of telegraphic outfits. Just now Master Ralph is working on an electric lighting plant which he expects to have installed in his home and in working order before Thanksgiving. This lighting plant will be practical, and probably will be extended to a few neighboring houses in the near future.

About two years ago Ralph prevailed upon his father to build him a shop in the back yard of his home. This shop is equipped with a three-horse gasoline engine, which is used to operate lathes, saws and other machinery. It will also furnish the power to run the dynamo that lights the house. There is a work bench of regular size and a complete outfit of tools for working in both wood and iron. These tools are kept in perfect condition, and are keen and bright. There are dynamos in this shop from the smallest size to the practical, powerful kind. Some of them were made by this young electrician, while others were purchased for some special purpose. There are magnets and switches and buttons and coils and half a hundred other articles and appliances which are used in his electrical experiments. Everything about the shop is in perfect order, and almost any tool could be found in the dark if necessary. Ralph has fitted up an electrical call bell, so that his mother needs but push a button in the kitchen to summon him from his work.

About a year ago Ralph became deeply interested in the subject of automobiles, and read everything he could find on the subject. He made up his mind that he would build one for himself, and when school closed last spring he proceeded to put his plan into effect. He found a discarded gasoline engine in the scrap pile at a factory. He asked for it, and it was turned over to him. He worked on this engine, and when through with it there was little resemblance to its former appearance. It was practically new and worked perfectly. The vehicle proper was built after the style of the runabout carriages seen so frequently on city streets. It is very graceful in appearance, and in size is about as large as other automobiles designed to carry two or three persons. The steering device and fuel and water tanks on the machine were designed and constructed by himself.

After many weeks of hard work the machine was finally completed, and the trial trip was a happy experience for Ralph. The machine worked perfectly, and was used almost daily on the village streets and country roads. It will probably be exhibited at the St. Louis Exposition next year as the work of the youngest automobile builder in the world.

A remarkable recognition of Ralph's attainments in the line of mechanics occurred last year, when he was 11 years old. He was invited by the Superintendent of the High School to sit in the class of advanced students that was studying physics and kindred subjects. His clear explanation of methods and principles frequently astonished his instructor and associates.

Ralph frequently visits his father's factory, where he has free scope. He can operate any of the machines and turn off work as skillfully as many old employes.

He is also very expert in operating the railway inspection cars that are made at the factory, and he is often taken along on experimental trips to look after the machines.

Ralph is a student in the town schools and attends regularly. His taste for literature runs after the lives and accomplishments of great men, notably Fulton, Morse and Edison.

The Cincinnati Enquirer, *November 19, 1902.*

Many years later Ralph commented on the little car in *The Circle* newsletter to Perfect Circle employees:

*The most remarkable thing about the car Dan and I built was that it ran—if the hills weren't too steep and the distance we drove wasn't too great.*

*Its motor was one of the single cylinder engines the Light Inspection Car Company was developing for the railroad motor cars. The car had only one speed forward and no reverse. On the steeper hills the passenger always had to bolster the engine's horsepower with plenty of pushing. And whenever we had to reverse, it was necessary to push it backwards.*

*The most common trouble we had with it occurred when it got going too fast—over 12 miles per hour. The chain would jump off the sprocket and would have to be put back before we could go on. This meant climbing underneath and threading the chain back in while someone pushed the car backwards.*

*The car was very noisy and scared the horses on the road so badly we were not permitted to drive the car when the horses were out. Dan and I, therefore, would get up at 3:00 A.M., get the car started about daylight, and drive it around until the horse-drawn vehicles appeared in the road.*

*Despite these many obstacles and the many practical weaknesses of the little car, it provided a lot of fun and experience for a couple of kids.*

How much did Ralph actually drive this car? Probably more than his parents knew or approved of. As has been said, he had learned to walk or run all over town by himself, determining where he was by the echo of his footsteps from the sides of buildings, trees or other landmarks. When there was no traffic he could drive through familiar territory in a similar way with the car. Dan did mention to his son Jack that the boys constructed an overhead line which was used to direct the car along a path, enabling Ralph to drive the car alone. Ralph never mentioned using such a device, but the car was obviously a great satisfaction to him. Not too long after he built the car he wanted to build a motorcycle. This project was vetoed by his father to Ralph's disappointment.

In 1904 a World's Fair was held in Saint Louis to commemorate the centennial of the Louisiana Purchase (later beautifully portrayed for many people in the movie *Meet Me in Saint Louis*). The fair was a showcase of American industrial progress and a thrill to the young entrepreneurs from Hagerstown. Ralph, now fourteen, his father, his Uncle Charlie Teeter, and Charlie's two small sons, Lothair and Macy, reveled in the opportunities to learn from the greatest mechanical geniuses in the world. Lothair, seven years old at the time, later related the following episode to his children: "One of the most spectacular exhibits in the Hall of Science and Industry was a gigantic steam engine two stories high. Ralph had learned to 'see' with his hands so Charlie, not noticing a small sign saying DO NOT TOUCH, held Ralph up to the machine so he could feel it, whereupon a burly engineer rushed over to them and roughly told them to get away. Embarrassed and chagrined, they complied. When the engineer became aware of Ralph's reason for touching the machine, his anger disappeared and he immediately apologized. With tears in his eyes he took Ralph in his arms and held him up high so the boy could examine every detail of the great machine. He kept the Teeters with him most of the afternoon, acting as their guide to the other exhibits and later taking them to dinner."

Displayed in the automotive section of the fair were a hundred and sixty different kinds of automobiles. What incredible progress had been made from the lone horseless carriage exhibited in the Columbian Exposition in Chicago just eleven years before! Nor were the Teeters outclassed: they entered the gasoline engine that Charlie had made for the cycle car into the fair competition, and they won a gold medal.

The importance to Ralph of the large family which surrounded him cannot be overemphasized. There were some twenty households of Teeters; and this did not include Ralph's seventeen uncles and aunts on his mother's side. John and Kate's social life centered around family concerns and gatherings. Many of these cousins would play very important roles in Ralph's future. Dan Teetor, the second cousin who helped build the little car, was always a close friend and support. George Keagy, Dick Waltz, and Neva Deardorff, all first cousins, spent much time with Ralph in college. Dick and George roomed with Ralph at different times, attending classes themselves and making Ralph's attendance at the university possible, as well as being a part of other important events in Ralph's life. Lothair, Macy, Don, Herman, and Winnie, all children of Ralph's Uncle Charlie, were younger than Ralph, but would be business associates and social companions throughout most of his life. Second cousins Ivan, Ray, and Bert Teetor would assist him later with many of his mechanical creations. Mabel Teetor Davis, her husband Leslie, and many more would be supportive family too. Ralph did not face the future alone.

Ralph entered high school with continuing enthusiasm for an engineering career. He was determined to learn everything he could about mechanics. To work through geometry and later trigonometry, he drove nails in parallel rows into a large square board and used rubber bands to graph the shapes and angles. He worked out various measuring devices using notches or audible clicks. He learned to type but he refused to learn Braille. He enjoyed a lively social life and did have some dates.

By Ralph's junior year in high school, basketball was still a new sport, but it was fast becoming popular around Indiana. In the fall of 1906 Hagerstown High School acquired a couple of basketballs, and the boys built a goal on two posts in the school yard. Deciding that was not good enough, the boys found that the brand new Knights of Pithias building had a large room, and convinced the owners to rent it to them so they could play basketball. Ralph had the basketball goals made at the factory and helped install them in the room. As the boys started shooting free throws, Ralph said to one of them, "I'll bet you I can do that too."

"You can't do it. It's all we can do to hit it when we can see it," challenged a classmate.

Ralph replied, "Okay, you show me where I should stand facing the basket with my feet right at the foul line and I will just show you."

When Ralph told the story as an adult he would always explain that he knew the distance from the foul line to the goal was fifteen feet and the height of the basket was ten feet (after all, they had just put up the goal) so it was a simple matter to estimate how high and hard he must throw the ball to make it traverse the necessary arc in order to go through the basket. His first attempt whooshed cleanly through the hoop.

The boys were aghast. "I can't believe it. Bet you can't do that again," someone dared.

"Sure I can, just watch," Ralph confidently replied. The ball touched the rim this time but it still went through.

"Do it once more!" begged an incredulous teammate.

"No sir!" replied Ralph. "I showed you I can do it and that's all." The truth was that he was almost as surprised at his success as were his teammates. That group of boys practicing in the Knights of Columbus Hall formed the first basketball team of Hagerstown High School. The next year, with Ralph Teeter as student manager, they played a number of teams from other towns in the area.

High school graduation came April 16, 1908. Commencement exercises were held on the second floor of the Oddfellows Hall on Main Street. Ralph, who by this time had wired both his workshop and his home for electric lights from a generator that he built in his workshop, created Hagerstown's first electrically lighted sign for his graduation. The numbers "1908" brightly glowed on the wall above the heads of the fourteen graduates who were seated on the stage. He described the event at a meeting of the Hagerstown Historical Society sixty-six years later. In doing so he also traced the history of electricity in Hagerstown.

The need for power at the factory had actually dictated bringing electricity to the town. At the turn of the century the only industries in Hagerstown were the milling complex which served the agricultural community and the Light Inspection Car Company, employing a dozen men. These enterprises could manage well on the power they drew from abundant natural gas in the local wells. But by 1907 the Light Inspection Car Company had grown to about twenty-five employees and the need for more power was growing too. Electricity was a must. It seemed to make some sense to include the rest of the town in this power expansion, since the town residents could use the elec-

tricity for lights in the evening after the factory was closed. The proposal for wiring the homes for electricity was put to a town vote, and
with only nominal objection the referendum passed.

Charlie's brother Henry, who knew something about gas engines,
was sent to Ohio to purchase an engine of suitable size. He returned
with a secondhand, eighty-five horsepower gas engine which was connected to a two-hundred-and-twenty-volt direct current generator to
furnish the power for the town and the factory. By Ralph's graduation, the system had been tested, but wires had not yet been run to
the homes. Ralph, of course, had been aware of every step of this
electrical project and knew just how it worked. He proposed to his
class that they should have the first electric sign in Hagerstown. Of
course they agreed. So he purchased light bulbs to outline the numbers, designed the sign, and had it made at the factory. Fortunately,
his commencement was held next door to the new generator. He ran
the wires from the sign out the window, across an alley and into the
building where the generator was run for the first time, just for that
evening.

Soon after that the homes were connected and electricity was
available from sundown to eleven o'clock at night. After women began purchasing electric irons, Tuesday morning was added to the power
schedule for ironing. Eventually power was available all day, but the
eleven o'clock curfew remained in effect well into the 1920s.


Ralph remembered his high school days as a happy time in his
life, the years full of fun. After graduation, his next challenge would
naturally be college. Never mind that this small village school had
not even offered all the English courses most colleges required for
admission; he was determined. He wanted to be a mechanical engineer, and to do that he needed a college education. Still, he admitted
to harboring some doubts about how he was going to be able to accomplish this; there weren't many folks in Hagerstown who had even
completed high school. The encouragement of one of his cousins
spurred Ralph on. Neva Deardorff, the daughter of his father's sister,
was graduating from the University of Michigan later the same spring.

She assured Ralph that he could manage college, suggesting that he come to her graduation and talk to the admissions department about enrolling in the university's engineering school. Ralph and his parents did travel to Ann Arbor for Neva's graduation and he applied for admission. He was told, however, that although the university would like to grant him admission, they didn't see any way they could teach him engineering, and they didn't think he could master the course of study.

Ralph attempted to persuade them. "I can't do it if I don't have a chance to try," he argued. But it was to no avail. The University of Michigan would not give him the opportunity.

By the time Neva left Michigan, she had been awarded a fellowship to the University of Pennsylvania for the next fall. This cousin still had faith in Ralph's ability and was determined that he would get the chance to study engineering which he so much wanted. Neva and Ralph talked and planned that summer. In the fall when Neva arrived in Philadelphia a week before school began, she talked with the admissions people there. Then she telephoned Ralph and told him to come. They were willing to listen to his story. So Ralph boarded the train for Philadelphia, having packed his trunk to stay for the semester. Neva met him and took him to the university. After progressing through the regular admissions procedure, Ralph was told that to be admitted he would have to gain the approval of Professor Henry W. Spangler, dean of the engineering school. Dean Spangler was a practical man who had been commander of one of the gunboats in the Spanish American War before coming to the University of Pennsylvania. He had the reputation of being compassionate and fair.

The dean listened to Ralph plead his case. Ralph pointed out that he already knew the mechanical part of the course because he had been using all the machines for years. With some tutoring in theory and other academics, he was sure he could complete the rest of the requirements for the degree.

Dean Spangler replied that he needed to consult his colleagues before making the decision. He had planned to meet with the faculty later that afternoon. "Come back at ten o'clock tomorrow morning and I'll give you an answer," he said.

Decades later Ralph would tell this story calmly and matter-of-factly, but one can only imagine the suspenseful anticipation he must have felt that first night in Philadelphia. He was not late for the ten o'clock appointment. Dean Spangler greeted him with the words, "Well, Teeter, we have decided to let you try it."

"I couldn't ask for more than that, and I sure appreciate it," was Ralph's delighted reply.

Dean Spangler continued, "You come to my house Sunday afternoon when we will have plenty of time to plan your classes and work out tutoring. I know some pretty smart seniors who I think would like to make a couple of dollars tutoring you. We will give it a try."

Ralph was not promised a degree; he was, instead, admitted as a special student. This special status was required not only because of his blindness, but also because of the deficiencies in preparatory courses from his country high school. In spite of this, he was to prove himself not only an adequate student but an exceptional one. At that time the University of Pennsylvania had a policy that the upper third of any class was not required to take the final examination at the end of the semester. Ralph succeeded in completing his entire four years without ever taking a final examination.

He remembered those years, too, as good ones. He lived close to the campus in a rooming house located among the fraternity houses. Each year one of his cousins from home, usually Dick Waltz or George Keagy, lived with him, reading his lessons to him while also taking courses at the university. Ralph learned to enjoy classical music by attending the theater, symphony, and opera in Philadelphia—students could purchase seats in the top of the balcony for fifty cents. He also joined the Whitney Engineering Society, a student organization at the university, and served as mechanical editor of its magazine, authoring two articles. One, entitled "The Use of the Manograph Indicator," appeared his junior year and the other, "The High Speed Internal Combustion Motor," was featured in the December issue of his senior year. The papers are technical, but his descriptions are graphically clear, and if one understands the vocabulary one can rather easily visualize the processes he described:

### The Use of the Manograph Indicator

The tendency in the last few years has been towards the increased speed of certain types of engines, especially those operated by internal combustion for automobile and light marine work. The speeds run so high in these machines that the ordinary drum indicator is totally inefficient for test work. The inertia of the moving parts of these is so great that the overtravel of the drum and the pencil mechanism would introduce enormous errors.

The manograph is an instrument designed for this sort of work. Its purpose is essentially that of the drum type of indicator. That is, to draw a diagram showing exactly what is taking place inside the cylinder at all parts of the cycle. It essentially consists of a small vertical cylinder in which a piston has been fitted and equipped with a spring. Around the cylinder is fitted a sleeve which is allowed to turn freely. This sleeve carries two vertical arms diametrically opposite and projecting above the top of the cylinder. A delicate mirror is mounted on a horizontal shaft, whose ends terminate in pivot bearings carried by these vertical arms. There is a light connecting rod, one end of which is fastened to a short arm projecting from the back of the mirror, the other, to the top of the piston. The sleeve carrying the mirror is rotated in alternate directions through a small angle by an arm projecting from the side. This arm is vibrated in a horizontal plane by means of a connecting rod running to some type of positively actuated reducing rig.

It is easily seen that an exact reproduction of the motion of the piston is transmitted through the reducing rig and connecting rod to the end of the arm on the outside of the sleeve surrounding the cylinder . . .

### The High Speed Internal Combustion Motor

At the time the automobile was first created, all internal combustion engines existing were of the heavy duty, slow speed type, and were not adapted to the propulsion of the motor car. However, the designers and experimenters saw the possibilities of these principles if they could be successfully embodied in a high speed, lightweight machine, so their attention was turned towards development along these lines. Many difficult problems entered with the increase of speed and flexibility. Some of these were ignition, carburetion, radiation, and lubrication. Some trouble was experienced from the rapidly reciprocating parts—valves, valve gearing, etc. While many *of the difficulties have not yet been entirely overcome, the improvement has been such that we have a practical power plant that can be operated successfully by anyone with average intelligence.*

*The two and four-cycle machines have so far survived the experimental stages. The inability to improve the poor regulation and the lower efficiency of the two-cycle type has greatly retarded its adoption, Its lower efficiency is probably due to the crowding of the cycle into two strokes . . .*

It was clear that Ralph Teeter's interests lay with automotive engines. It is possible that he brought more practical knowledge of such engines from Hagerstown, Indiana, to the university than he actually learned there. The principles and theories of engineering which he mastered at the university, however, were vital to his future career.

At the end of his junior year Ralph again went to Dean Spangler, this time to plan his senior year and, for the first time, to discuss graduation. Ralph had determined that, in spite of the university's original plan for him to proceed through as a non-degree student, he would be able to fulfill all the requirements for a mechanical engineering degree. He really desired the degree and asked Dean Spangler what he could do to earn it.

Ralph acknowledged that there was one requirement that he could not complete: the course in mechanical drawing. Dean Spangler assured him that he was not at all concerned about the mechanical drawing requirement, because Ralph had demonstrated complete understanding of the subject. Then he asked, "Teeter, do you remember when you first came to my office to apply for admission, I told you to come back the next day after I had talked with the faculty?"

"I'll never forget it," Ralph answered.

"Did I ever tell you what we decided in that faculty meeting that afternoon?" pressed Spangler with a smile.

"I only remember that you said that you would give me a chance to try it," Ralph replied.

Dean Spangler's smile widened. "Do you know why we told you that? We all knew you couldn't do it. But we agreed that it would be kinder if you found that out for yourself than for us to tell you. We were sure that we would not be bothered with you for more than two weeks."

Ralph had proven them all wrong. On his return to the University of Pennsylvania for his senior year, Ralph was officially a senior candidate for graduation. But near the end of the year he was called into the office of a new dean of engineering, where he was confronted by an obviously upset man. "I have terrible news for you, Ralph. It has been brought to my attention that you have not made the graphs and charts required for graduation. There is a rule that each student must complete those graphs for himself. No one can do it for you, and I just don't see how we can allow you to graduate without them." Needless to say, Ralph was crushed. He went back to his room and lay awake all night trying to think what he could do to fulfill this final requirement. By morning he had a idea. Meeting the dean as he entered his office, Ralph presented his plan. The dean listened. "If you can do that, Ralph, we will accept it," he replied.

Ralph, with the help of his roommate, purchased pieces of screen wire that were just the same size grid as graph paper and had them framed to hold their shape. Then he diligently wove pieces of colored wire through the holes, counting off the spaces to make the charts. He wove them up and down to make bar graphs and across the screen for the line graphs. When he was finished he presented them to the dean. As Ralph told it later, he said, "I'm sure the dean was crying and so was I."

Ralph graduated with a Bachelor of Science in Mechanical Engineering on Wednesday, June 19, 1912, in the Metropolitan Opera House in Philadelphia. His only regret was that his good friend and mentor, Dean Spangler, was not there to share his victory. This fine educator had died of a heart attack the summer before while fishing in Maine.

Ralph enjoyed relating at least the first part of this story, even though it required him to speak of the blindness which otherwise he did not often acknowledge. Furthermore, it delighted him that the University of Pennsylvania admitted "quite a few" more blind students who successfully earned their engineering degrees after he had proven that it could be done. He was always grateful to the

University of Pennsylvania for risking the time and effort to give him his chance to succeed and to chart the course for others.

Ralph Teetor's relationship with his alma mater was to prove an enduring one. He returned to the Philadelphia campus June 18, 1930, to receive the Master of Mechanical Engineering Degree. He was honored in 1937 by the Engineering Alumni Society of the University in Philadelphia and gave the keynote speech titled "Progress in the Automotive Industry and Development of the Diesel Engines." Four years later Tau Beta Pi, honorary fraternity of engineers, elected Ralph to membership. In 1976 the Engineering School created the Gallery of Distinguished Engineering Alumni at the University of Pennsylvania, composed of the portrait of one outstanding alumnus from each branch of engineering. The press announcement stated:

*The new gallery has been established to honor living alumni for their career contributions to encourage today's engineering students to develop their individual talents to the fullest, to sharpen their sensitivity to the needs of society, and to blend these qualities in exciting careers as responsible citizens.*

Ralph Teetor was the first alumnus to be selected for that gallery. Eighty-six years old and somewhat crippled with arthritis, he chose not to attend the ceremony but was represented by his daughter, son-in-law, and grandson, also named Ralph. It was a perfect closure to a very rewarding relationship with the university which had once favored him and which he continued to favor the rest of his life.

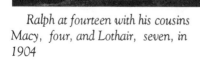

*Ralph at fourteen with his cousins Macy, four, and Lothair, seven, in 1904*

*Ralph, twelve years old, 1902.*

*Ralph in the automobile that he and Dan built, 1902.*

*Ralph in his workshop, building his steam engine, 1902. Insert — the steam engine which still runs.*

1907–08 Hagerstown High School's basketball team played its first competetive season. Ralph (student manager) is second from left on the back row. (Courtesy of Donald McCullough)

*A Teeter Family Reunion in 1905. Left to right: (Back row) Elizabeth Deardorff, Neva Deardorff, Leora Teeter, Josie Teeter, Mable Teeter, George Keagy, Mary Keagy, Charles Teeter, Donald Teeter, Kate Teeter. (Front row) Zachariah Teeter, Minnie Teeter, Lothair Teeter (child), Ralph Teeter, Henry Teeter, Joe Teeter, Henry Keagy, John Teeter, Macy Teeter, Frank Teeter.*

# Establishing His Credentials

Many changes had taken place at the Light Inspection Car Company while Ralph was busy in high school and college. Charlie had continued to improve the single-cylinder engine for the inspection car. Sales had grown so much by 1905 that although most of the income was reinvested in the company, the investors began taking some small dividends. The crude, secondhand machinery of twenty years before was being replaced with larger, more powerful equipment, most of it built right at the factory.

The company's first plunge into the automobile business came during 1905. Although Ralph was only a sophomore in high school at the time, he had been so involved in this project that he was able to remember it clearly sixty years later in a letter replying to inquiries of Walter Seeley, an antique car collector who was restoring an American car:

*To my knowledge there is no other person living today who can remember in detail the information you asked about the American Underslung Car. The engines in your car were built by the Teetor-Hartley Motor Company, but at the time those engines were built it was the Light Inspection Car Company, and the company's name was not changed to Teetor-Hartley Motor Company until 1914. In 1905 two men, a Mr. Menasco and Mr. V. A. Longacre, had made what would then be considered a fortune in the lumber business in the Northwest. They then decided that they would go into the automobile manufacturing business, and since Indianapolis, Indiana, at that time claimed more successful automobile companies than any other city in the country, they came there to start their business.*

*For their chief engineer they employed Fred Tone, who had been the assistant chief engineer with Marion Motor Car Company. The design for their first car was quite conventional for the time. Instead of manufacturing the components, they purchased the axles, transmissions, drive lines, steering gears, engines, etc., and assembled the cars from these units as a great many other automobile companies did at that time. Having determined that the engine made by the Continental Company best suited their requirements, they approached Continental to purchase these engines. However Continental had just accepted a substantial contract with Hudson Automobile Company and did not have any capacity to furnish completed engines to American. Continental told American that their vendors could provide some of the principle parts if the American Company could find some machine shop which could make some of the smaller parts, machine the castings, assemble and test the engines.*

*Fred Tone knew the Teetors at the Light Inspection Car Company, so he and Mr. Longacre asked Charlie and John if they could finish and test the Continental engines. The Teetors' machine shop was small, employing no more than twenty-five people. They explained that they had never built anything more than a small single-cylinder gasoline engine and knew nothing about manufacturing four-cylinder engines. However, the American folks explained that they would need only twenty-five or thirty engines the first year so the Teetors agreed to tackle the job . . .*

So the company began to build four-cylinder engines for the American cars. A few years later Charles Teeter secured a contract from John Willys, president of the Willys-Overland Company of Indianapolis to machine the cylinders for their motors, at the rate of about forty-eight cylinders a day. This was quite a contract for its time, for few manufacturers were making as many as twelve cars a day.

With this experience the Teeters entered the automobile industry. They continued to make engines for the American Motor Company until its demise in 1914. After learning how to make multiple-cylinder engines, Charlie and his assistants started improving the engines with their own designs, naming these Teeter engines, later Teetor-Hartley, and sold their own engines to American and several other automobile companies.

Cooperative engineering built strong friendships between the engineers at American and their counterparts in Hagerstown. Ralph loved American cars, particularly the sporty Underslung. Interestingly, this style was designed almost by accident. In 1907 when the frames were delivered to the American Company, they were unloaded upside down. Seeing them in this position gave Fred Tone the idea to make a lower, sporty roadster by mounting the frame upside down with the axles over the frame. They called these new models "underslung" and they became a big hit. American built all their roadsters underslung, while continuing to make sedans conventionally "overslung" until they went out of business in 1913. Ralph's father purchased a 1909 Overslung seven-passenger touring car, equipped, of course, with a Teeter engine. Ralph continued to describe his love affair with the American car to the inquiring Mr. Seeley:

*The next car was a 1912 four-passenger American 30 Underslung that my father gave me for a college graduation present, in June of 1912. All of the Model 30s were equipped with Teetor-Hartley 4 x 5-inch four-cylinder engines which had all cylinders cast in a block with valve arrangements known as a T-Head; that is, all exhaust valves on one side and all intakes on the other. Each set of valves was operated by their own cam shafts located on each side of the crankcase.*

*The last car I purchased was a 1914 seven-passenger Model 66 Underslung touring car. I believe it was designed for the 1914 catalog, but the company never operated through 1914. My car was the last one ever built and was finished between the time that the American Company was sold to the Winternitz Wrecking Company and the time they wrecked and sold the plant piecemeal at public sale. My car was painted a brilliant lavender and was powered with our new 4 x 6-inch six-cylinder Teetor-Hartley engine. It was a beautiful automobile, and my friends referred to it as my Lavender Chariot.*

*I remember that the Winternitz Company bought all of the physical assets of American for $100,000. I have never wanted to have $100,000 to spend so badly in my life, as I did want to buy that company. I was only then a little more than a year out of college, and at that age, was sure that I was smart enough to pull it out of its financial difficulties. I do believe that* *the American Underslung cars had the most dramatic appeal of any cars that were ever built, and ever since that company failed, have wished it could have survived.*

In 1912, the Light Inspection Car Company began building engines for the McFarlan, built in Connersville. The McFarlan was one of the finer cars of its time, each unit individually built with many custom features. Ralph carried the custom work an extra step.

*In 1915, being a typical young man, I wanted a three-passenger roadster. I was not interested in as large a car as the McFarlan, so I had assembled a smaller chassis made principally of Auburn automobile parts with a smaller six-cylinder Teetor engine. McFarlan then built the special body and fenders, and completed the car according to my design. It was a beautiful job and attracted all the attention that was desired.*

Ralph wrote this originally in a letter to Al Arnheim and then repeated it in the preface to Arnheim's *What Was the McFarlan?* He continued in a letter to Arnheim:

*I used the car until 1918 when I took a temporary war job with the New York Shipbuilding Corporation in Camden, and lived in Philadelphia. I sold the car while there and never have heard of it since. I would now give most anything to have kept it, for it was not only a beautiful job but was quite unusual.*

*Harry McFarlan was, of course, the only person by the name who was active in the business. However, Bert Barrows was the general manager and the man with whom we had most of our business association. A short time before McFarlan quit the business, Bert Barrows stepped into an open freight elevator shaft and fell to his death. The automatic safety gate had failed to drop into position when the elevator left the upper floor.*

Ralph grieved for his friend, but the accident itself also frightened him. He cautioned all whom he loved to be sure to see that the elevator was actually there before stepping through the open door.

Working conditions in the little factory at the turn of the century were primitive by later standards. Charles Thornburg discussed the days when he worked at Railway Inspection Car Manufacturing Company for five cents an hour. He had begun in 1899 and worked through the years when John Teetor was president but Charles Teetor was in charge of manufacturing:

*We always worked sixty hours a week and in my pay envelope every week I found three dollars . . . Our Tool Room was wide open to everyone and everything. We had considerable trouble with dogs running through and visiting our different machines. But Mr. C. N. Teetor [Charlie] found a way to discourage the visiting dogs. He had an old dog named Noble weighing 160 pounds. He parked him in the Tool Room and every time one of the visiting dogs would enter the room, old Noble would grab him by the back of the neck and throw him into the air. After a few such treatments, the dog business was on the downgrade.*

*I was asked the question "Why are you still working here?" and can answer sincerely by using one man's name: C. N. Teetor. It seemed that he had little ways of doing things for employees that made them respect him. It wasn't unusual for Mr. Teetor to bring down a jar of lemonade during hot summer days. Several times during the summer he would take the entire group picnicking. He would pay all the expenses himself and was with us in any kind of game or contest that took place.*

*Any time disaster struck our homes, Mr. Teetor was always one of the first there to assist us . . .*

Another worker, Grover Brower recounted:

*I started to work here September 10, 1906. I left a nine-dollar-per week job at the Gar Scott Company of Richmond, Indiana, to come to Perfect Circle to work for five cents an hour and learn the machinist trade.*

*After working here two weeks I was raised to seven cents per hour. At the end of one year I was getting ten cents per hour or one dollar per day.*

*There have been several who have worked with this organization that I term real men. Among these were Charles, Frank, and Joe Teetor [all brothers] They knew how to get the work out and how to get along with employees. They could always see the underdog's side of the story and were always willing to help him. I firmly believe the younger Teetor boys are trying to follow in the footsteps of their father and uncles.*

Erville Gray, after thirty-two years with the company, wrote:

*Like most of the older employees, I worked on a farm prior to my employment with the Company. May 2, 1912, I was hired to turn and cut piston rings. I have spent most of my employment with the Company on a turning lathe. The past two years I have been on the guard force.*

*One time I was sent to Bob Thurston's department and came across Pete Dalby, who has a horror of mice. The boys in the department seemed to delight in putting a live mouse in the drawer of Pete's bench. Upon discovery of the rodent, Pete would start running and wouldn't stop until he was out of the shop. Anyone trying to stop him was slugged on the spot. Pete's fellow workers never seemed to tire of the joke, but management did. So it was stopped.*

*In those days everyone was a fireman. For our heat, we had ordinary stoves and everyone had to take turns firing our heating system. If this responsibility was shirked, drastic measures were taken.*

*'Dad' [Charlie] Teetor seldom let a load of watermelons get by the plant. He would buy the entire load and shut the place down so everybody could enjoy the melons with him.*

(Reprinted from interviews in *The Circle*, the Perfect Circle employee newsletter.)

Charles Teeter was often called "C. N." or "Dad" by friends and employees. The sixty hours per week which Charles insisted on comprised a standard workweek everywhere. The pay was not particularly good for the time, (although wages were usually increased to twenty-five cents an hour when a man married) but the hard physical labor was lightened by the considerable kidding and horseplay. Most importantly, all accounts of the first forty years of the company describe an intense loyalty and a camaraderie among all the employees and management, specifically credited to Charlie's leadership. The men knew that "Dad" worked harder and longer hours than any of them. They watched him invent and improve the products that they were making, and they knew that he cared about them.

Hourly pay for members of the family wasn't much higher than that of other employees, but the family stockholders did pay themselves generous dividends as the company became more profitable. John gave Ralph one-half share of his stock, Ralph's first ownership in the company, when Ralph graduated from high school in 1908 and another one-half a year later.

Ralph returned to Hagerstown following graduation from college in 1912. He lived with his parents and worked each day at the little Light Inspection Car Company. There is no record of a job description or wages, but since Charlie had a tendency to set pay scales for employees more in accordance with what they *needed* than what they were *worth*, one can assume Ralph's wages were modest. It is known that Ralph and Charlie worked closely together, developing and improving the new engines. Just how many of the ideas were Ralph's and how many were Charlie's no one will ever know. It's doubtful that they knew themselves. They had one technical argument that lasted several weeks over the design of a water pump. Charlie was a water wheel enthusiast and he had designed the water circulating pump on the automobile engine like a water wheel. He piped both the inlet and outlet of the pump to the outside race of the pump housing, thinking that the impeller would pick up the water from one side and exhaust it from the opposite side. Ralph maintained that it would not work because of Newton's Laws of Motion. Ralph was right and they redesigned the pump to bring the water into the center of the impeller.

Although the Light Inspection Car Company continued profitably shipping the little cars all over the world, the engine sales were growing even faster, making that business much more interesting and economically promising. In 1913 the board of directors, made up of mostly Teeters and Hartleys, changed the name of the company to Teetor-Hartley Motor Company. The spelling change in the company name required another change in the family name. The Teetor family in and around Hagerstown was much larger than just the descendants of Zachariah. Zachariah had three brothers who lived nearby, and they had children. Part of the Teeters were now spelling their names with an "-or." Some said that it had been misspelled on a land grant and it was easier to change the name than the land grant. Whatever the reason, the family decided that the time had come to standardize the spelling. Charlie's wife, Leora, convinced Charlie that the name looked much better and more sophisticated with "-or" instead of "-er." So he held out for that spelling and on January 1, 1914, all the family changed the spelling of their names from Teeter to Teetor and so it remained, except occasionally in the next few weeks, when someone forgot and signed his name the old way. On that day also the company became the Teetor-Hartley Motor Company with the same company management; John was president, Charlie general manager, and the rest of the family stockholders, making up the board of directors.

Ralph and his Uncle Charlie were at this time deeply engrossed in engineering improvements. They had found that a very strategic part of engine performance was the process inside the cylinder where the fuel ignited, causing the piston to slide back and forth. The key to effective combustion is the ring of metal around the piston, which seals the inside of the cylinder as the piston slides back and forth. Better piston rings would mean more efficient and powerful engines. The focus of Ralph and Charlie's improvements, therefore, centered on piston rings. Soon the automotive world began to recognize that the Teetor piston ring was superior and it was appearing in cars made by Auburn, Pilot, Davis, McFarlan, Westcott, Staver-Chicago, Empire, Lexington, and Willys.

The noise of war in Europe began to reverberate all across the United States. Soon Ralph's friends and associates were signing up to fight "the war to end all wars." As he waved good-bye to friends and relatives leaving for the Army and Navy, Ralph sadly felt left behind. Finally, early in 1918, a good friend, Wilfred Jessup, accepted a call to serve on a military project which was located in Philadelphia. Ralph asked if Will could find him a job in which Ralph's experience as an engineer could be used in spite of his lack of vision. After much inquiry, probably even some persuasion, the general manager of the New York Shipbuilding Corporation in Camden, New Jersey, agreed to take Ralph into his office as an advisor for mechanical problems. The truth was that the man did not have the slightest idea what he was going to do with Ralph. Although there was no salary offered, Ralph accepted the opportunity. He lived with his cousin, Dick Waltz, who was stationed in the naval shipyard there and was assisted by another cousin, George Keagy.

The first few days must have been discouraging; the young engineer was given nothing to do. Then he learned that the company had a contract with the Navy to produce twenty new twin-propeller torpedo-boat destroyers, 318 feet in length. In order to operate at the required speed of thirty-five knots, these ships had to be equipped with more powerful engines than had ever been used in such boats before. Each of the two propellers was driven by a large steam turbine. If the rotors on these turbines were not perfectly balanced, they would shake the boat to pieces at high speeds. For months the engineers had been unable to balance these turbines accurately enough to be accepted by the Navy. The ships were badly needed for the war effort; German torpedo boats were causing serious damage to ships in the Atlantic.

Ralph understood the problem. Back in Hagerstown he had dynamically balanced crankshafts in high speed, four-cylinder Teetor-Hartley engines for race cars. He asked the New York Shipbuilding officials how they were trying to balance the rotors. They showed him the device mounted near the spinning shaft which marked the heavy side of the rotor as it passed the marker. Ralph reminded them that the mark would not be made at the exact heavy spot but a little beyond it, and if they would spin the rotors in the opposite direction and mark it again, the heavy spot would be exactly halfway between the two marks. It would then be relatively easy, by trial and error, to attach weight to the opposite side to bring the machine into balance.

The engineers objected, saying that they couldn't spin the rotors in the opposite direction, since the turbine was completely assembled and they were turning the rotor by steam pressure, the same way it was turned in a ship. There was no way to turn it in the opposite direction. The engineers had no faith in Ralph's plan. Ralph, however, asked for one assistant and an opportunity to attempt what he had proposed. With little to lose they condescendingly agreed to let the young man try.

He first took the turbines apart, removed the rotors, then mounted them on a shaft turned by an electric motor which could turn them in either direction. In the manner he had described to the Navy engineers, he spun the rotors clockwise, marking the heavy point, then counterclockwise, again marking the heavy point. Finding the midpoint, he applied balancing weight on the opposite side. In a few hours he had the first rotor balanced. Ralph's highly developed sense of touch did give him an advantage over the measuring gauges in use at the time for determining how much weight should be added to bring the rotors into perfect balance. The engineers were generous in their praise. Although the war was over before the torpedo-boat destroyers could be placed in combat, they were later sold to England and used extensively in World War II.

After the balanced turbines had been accepted by the Navy inspectors, Ralph asked to be put on the payroll. The superintendent told him that he was "too big a man" to go on the payroll, but that his case would be taken care of to his complete satisfaction. He became a consultant to the foremost engineers in American shipbuilding, but no record remains of what wages, if any, he was paid.

Following a visit with Ralph soon after his successful experiment, Wilfred Jessup wrote to John Teetor in Hagerstown:

*My dear Mr. Teetor,*

*Of course you have heard from Ralph and know how happy he is in the splendid work he has done at the New York Shipbuilding Corporation. I do not think I ever saw a happier man in my life than Ralph was Sunday. He put across a great big job and it was recognized by the men further up.*

*Some three weeks ago he and Dick came to my room and Ralph was terribly discouraged. I did all I could to reassure him and in the kindliest way pointed out that the proposition he had in mind* [his solution to the balancing problem] *was of course in entire opposition to all previous experience and practice but I did believe that his plan would work out. So it has occurred.*

*The finest thing about it, however, and the thing that encourages Ralph so much is that he not only has proven his capacity, but more than that, he has proven it among utter strangers. It is great encouragement to him now* to know that, in spite of his handicap, he can go out in the big, round world and, entirely divorced from the influence of friends, the recommendation of acquaintances or family associations, he can find a place in his profession where he can do real and constructive work with good compensation.

I wanted you to get this letter, if possible, on Thanksgiving to add just a little to the pleasure of the day for yourself and Mrs. Teetor.

With kindest regards,
Wilfred Jessup

One can be sure that John and Kate found a great deal to be thankful for on that Thanksgiving Day in 1918. The war ended and Ralph soon came home to praise and acclaim. The story of his accomplishment appeared in several newspapers around the country with some variation in accuracy. Found in Ralph's files was a newspaper clipping which described an interview with a Camden, New Jersey, reporter:

If soldiers who have lost their eyesight in the war could meet a young mechanical engineer, at present working for the New York Shipbuilding Corporation in Camden, they would take heart.

His courage and unselfishness are an inspiration to all who know him, his employers say. He is a young man who has fought a good fight and won . . .

He is twenty-eight, and in appearance is uncommonly robust. The impression he gives in general, is of power, health, and sanity . . . He enters with zest into outdoor exercise in whatever it is possible for him to participate.

"If those who have been seriously incapacitated and have before them what seem almost impossible readjustments to make, could realize that the mental attitude is everything, it would help them, I think," Ralph Teetor said today at lunch hour.

"Men with a handicap must begin to think what they can do for somebody else. And they must accept and follow up on every opportunity. One man I know lost his eyesight eight years ago, and he has not tried to do *anything. Anyone is happiest when doing the most good. As long as a man thinks about himself, he won't improve. Of course, he'll have to try all sorts of little devices. And he must not give up. There are thousands of things he can find to do. This is a day of specialization. So why bother with what cannot be done?"*

*Mr. Teetor insists that he is in no way unusual, not at all like Helen Keller, he says, who is "one of the extraordinary personalities of the age, a woman with a remarkable mind to begin with."*

*At any rate, he is one of the unusual individuals to whom the law of compensation has brought the power to concentrate and the secret of happiness.*

Ralph could give such advice with authority. There would be more testing. However, this victory was significant and the success exhilarating, for now he knew he could become a contributing member of society. He had shown that he could compete professionally in the sighted world without pity or coddling or special accommodations. He had earned his credentials as a mechanical engineer beyond the protective cocoon of family and school. Now he had the self confidence to move ahead into an automobile industry which was preparing to move into a new phase.

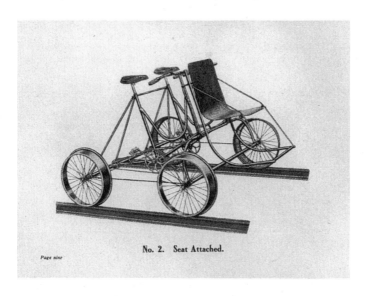

No. 2. Seat Attached.

*Page nine*

No. 5.

*Page seventeen*

*From the catalog of the Light Inspection Car Company, 1909.*

*Ralph and Dan Teetor pose in the newly designed Staver automobile about 1912. Dan was chief engineer for the Staver Carriage Company in Chicago. Ralph was designing the Teeter Motor (later Teetor-Hartley) used in the Staver. (Courtesy of Jack Teetor)*

Ralph and his parents check out their new 1909 American Overslung touring car in front of their home in Hagerstown. Such a car was obviously the object of much curiosity in the town.

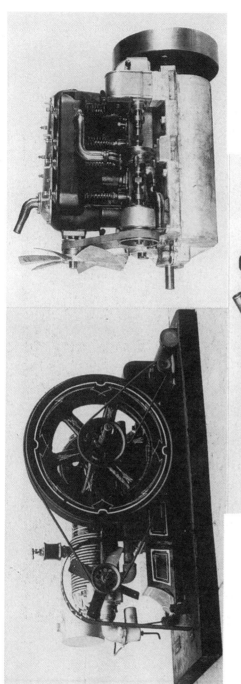

*A variety of Teetor-Hartley Engines, circa 1914.*

*Piston ring grinding at the Indiana Piston Ring Company about 1918. (Hagerstown Museum Collection)*

PEERLESS

WHITE

WILLY'S OVERLAND

MARMON

AMERICAN

CHEVROLET

PACKARD

Early Perfect Circle customers.

*Engine customers of Teetor-Hartley Engine Company, about 1914.*

# Coming of Age — The 1920s

Ralph returned from Philadelphia nearly a year later to a different company than the one he had left. He could hardly be surprised by the change; the basis of the next major phase of the company had begun before he had departed.

Although it was common practice for most early engine manufacturers to purchase component parts from outside sources, nearly every part of the Teetor-Hartley engine was machined in Hagerstown. Connecting rods, crankshafts, camshafts, valves, pistons, and piston rings all were manufactured by separate departments within the little factory. This policy of "don't buy it—make it" had permitted Teetor-Hartley to control costs and maintain high quality workmanship.

After Henry Ford's Model T made its debut in 1908 and revolutionized automotive manufacturing again in 1913 with the moving assembly line, the price of automobiles fell, creating formidable competition for small, hand machining auto plants. Automotive manufacturers scrambled to adapt the new cost-cutting assembly line technologies to their own production. The Teetors wisely recognized that their individually machined Teetor-Hartley motor was not adapted to the direction in which automotive manufacturing was moving. Already some of the companies producing hand-crafted cars, such as the American, were in financial trouble or had been forced out of business. The recession of the early 1920s would wipe out many more. And, too, the growth of the new, low-cost production methods was shifting the center of automobile manufacturing from Indianapolis to

Detroit, where raw material and capital were more readily obtainable.

It has been said that it is better to be lucky than wise. Certainly Charlie and John were wise enough in their perception that the future of the automotive industry lay outside customized engine manufacture. But luck was with them too: they were already producing a specialty automotive component which could successfully take them into the future they were envisioning. Because piston rings were the most complicated, highly-technical, significant components of an engine's performance, Charlie and Ralph had found them most interesting to improve. As a result, the piston rings Teetor-Hartley was making for its own motors were so superior that other automotive companies were purchasing their rings too. The company focused on what it could do well, jettisoning what looked less promising for the future. Teetor-Hartley got out of the faltering custom engine business and concentrated on the successful piston ring component. The engine business and the building it occupied were sold to Lexington Car Company of Connersville, Indiana, for five hundred thousand dollars. Teetor-Hartley kept the proprietary piston ring manufacturing for themselves, changing the company name at this time to Indiana Piston Ring Company.

The Lexington Company, later known as the Ansted Company, paid fifty thousand dollars cash at the time of the engine division sale and promised to pay the rest over three years. However, Lexington's business failed rapidly, and by 1921 they were bankrupt, having made only one more payment of twenty thousand dollars. This was no catastrophe for Indiana Piston Ring Company, because by this time the piston ring business had grown so large that the return of the manufacturing building and equipment in Hagerstown was even more valuable than the money would have been. The Indiana Piston Ring Company repossessed the building where they had formerly made engines, converted it to ring manufacturing, and continued to flourish. But now Ralph had another project in mind in which success was even more important.

Ralph was in love. In the fall of 1916 a new teacher was hired at Hagerstown High School to teach English and Latin. Nellie Van Antwerp had just graduated from Indiana University. She showed unusual independence of spirit in requesting a salary of eight dollars a week—the usual rate in Indiana for beginning teachers was a dollar less. "I intend to do a better job of teaching than the average person and I'm worth a dollar more," she told the superintendent. From all accounts she was right. Her reputation among her students was that she was strict, fair, and properly demanding, a fit partner for a young man "on his way up." Hagerstown's eligible bachelors gathered at the covered-dish socials at the Congregational Christian Church, where they could properly meet single young ladies who were new in town. Ralph and the attractive Nellie met among the au gratin potatoes and lemon pies. Nellie taught only one year in Hagerstown before she returned to her home in Huntington, Indiana, to teach four more years. She felt obligated to repay her father for the expense of her college education. Ralph pursued her with many automobile trips north before they were married five years later.

Nellie had grown up in a strict but loving family in Huntington, with a younger sister, Louise, and a half-brother, Lewis, fifteen years older. Her father, Theodore, was a tall, stern grocer who ruled his home with absolute authority. Her pretty mother, May, was fun-loving, even a bit impish, loved by all who knew her, but totally deferential to her husband.

May Van Antwerp was Theo's second wife; Hattie, his first wife, had died in 1880. When May married Theo in 1893 she was just twenty-three, sixteen years younger than her new husband and only nine years older than her somewhat mischievous, fourteen-year-old stepson, Lewis. Lewis was not about to be put under a mother's thumb at that stage in his life, but he came to adore his young, sister-like stepmother. Lewis's "Grandma Van," his father's mother, who had served as his mother most of his life, continued to live with them, smoothing ruffled feathers and baking big, soft, white sugar cookies and other treats for him and later, his sisters. There was little trace of "old country" influence in this home, for the families had been living in the United States for several generations. Nellie's ancestors fought in both the Revolution and the Civil War before settling in the north-eastern Indiana town of Huntington. Family lore maintained, not too proudly because of his historical reputation for ill-temper, that Peter Stuyvesant, who purchased Long Island, New York, from the Indians, was one of their ancestors.

Although Nellie's heritage qualified her for membership in the Daughters of the American Revolution, she refused to join. She was not interested in belonging to any organization which based its membership requirements solely on ancestry.

Ten months after Theo and May were married, Nellie was born. Her sister Louise arrived three years later. As a child Nellie was spirited, popular and obedient. Her father had strict ideas about how his daughters should behave; they were never allowed to roller skate or ride bicycles because he did not consider such activities to be lady-like. Nellie loved her father, accepting his authority without much question. She was a good student and persuaded her father to allow her to go to college. Her choice was Northwestern University in Evanston, Illinois, but Theo, who was not entirely convinced girls needed a college education at all, considered that Chicago-area school too expensive.

She enrolled in Indiana University in the fall of 1912, majoring in Latin and Greek. Her leadership skills developed in her sorority, Kappa Kappa Gamma, where she served two terms as president, the first time that chapter had reelected its head officer. Even though Nellie had a fine record at Indiana University, Theo permitted her sister Louise only a music education in Cincinnati rather than the university experience that she most desired. Many years later Theo's grandson and namesake remembered his grandfather as tall and erect. "I was almost afraid of him although he always treated me well," he said. Ted also remembered that his grandfather was an outspoken Republican.

After graduation in 1916 from Indiana University, Nellie came to Hagerstown to begin her first teaching position. Following that first covered-dish supper, Ralph invited her to go with him for an automobile ride through the countryside, his favorite dating pastime, with George Keagy and his wife Louise. As they began to spend time together, Nellie learned about the uncles and aunts and many cousins. She learned about his exceptional mechanical abilities and his preference for the Christian Science religion. And she learned to love and admire this brilliant young man. It had been a much more interesting winter teaching in this small town than she had anticipated when she first arrived.

She also had much to think about. Ralph did bring with him some unusual attributes. He would always wish to live in the small village of Hagerstown, offering her neither the privacy nor the sophistication that she was accustomed to in a larger town. And what about the very "different" religion of Christian Science, so difficult for her to embrace? Could she keep peace with all those relatives? How could she compete with his intense interest in tinkering in his workshop? Then there was his blindness: it had to be considered. Could she be the lifelong support of this man? The life that Ralph was proposing must have appeared to offer more than average risk.

Ralph traveled many times to Huntington over the next few years to convince Nellie that he was worth the risk. They were married December 30, 1922, and she never looked back. Reverend Ernest G. Mobley married the couple in the Van Antwerp home in Huntington with their parents, Dan and Charlotte Teetor, and George and Louise Keagy, among the guests. An altar flanked by bouquets of roses had been arranged in front of the fireplace in the parlor. Nellie, petite and trim, was a lovely young woman. Her wavy light brown hair was long enough that she could sit on it, but she always wore it neatly swirled on her head in a figure eight, creating a stunning effect. She did not wear a traditional white wedding gown, but for this simple ceremony chose instead a soft brown dress trimmed with a bit of fur. Ralph had ordered an orchid for Nellie's bridal bouquet because she had never had one of the exotic blooms, but it didn't arrive in time and a few roses had to be substituted at the last moment. For years Ralph presented Nellie with an orchid at every wedding anniversary and every Easter to compensate for that disappointment, a disappointment surely more poignant for Ralph than for Nellie. They honeymooned in French Lick, Indiana, and then settled in Hagerstown within the modest frame home of John and Kate, Ralph's parents, just two blocks from the factory.

Living with her in-laws was not easy for Nellie. Even though she made friends easily and found plenty to occupy herself, she must have missed her privacy and independence. But it was three years before she and Ralph achieved a measure of family independence by building a three-bedroom bungalow next door to Ralph's parents. It was the house which would be their home for the following eleven years.

Between college and marriage Ralph had pursued a hobby of building boats. Boat-building was a popular pastime for many of Ralph's engineering friends at that time; as these young adventurers continued to improve the gasoline engines for automobiles, they naturally extended their interest to boats. Just as racing was popular for testing automobiles, during warmer months boat races were frequently held on Midwestern lakes and rivers, especially around Detroit, to test and show off innovations. Both motorboats and sailboats intrigued Ralph, but during these years his greatest interest, not surprisingly, was seeing how fast he could make a motorboat go. Boat performance was complicated by variables such as the shape and trim of the boat hull, weight distribution, and size and pitch of the propeller. There was much to learn about boats; he converted an old barn about a block from his house into a workshop just to work on his boats. The first craft, a twenty-two foot planing speedboat, was probably built from a kit around 1914 and was powered with a four-cylinder Teetor-Hartley motor similar to the ones being installed in automobiles. Ralph tested the boat on Lake Wawasee, about one hundred miles north of Hagerstown. Several years later he bought a twenty-foot racing boat named *Miss Detroit,* built by Chris and Jay Smith (founders of the Chris Craft Boat Company) in Algonac, Michigan. Ralph and the Smiths had become good friends, engineering boat engines for speed and smooth performance.

By this time Ralph and his family had enjoyed several summer vacations at Lake Wawasee. Ralph brought the *Miss Detroit* to Wawasee to see how she would run on the smooth surface of the largest lake in Indiana. The boat held two people in the passenger compartment at the stern, just behind the huge marine engine. Her rudder was attached under the bow of the boat instead of the conventional place at the stern to enable her to make sharper turns. Among Ralph's friends and relatives, there was never a shortage of young hands willing to handle the steering controls. However, the sleek mahogany boat almost met its demise before it began. Preparing for their first ride and after much fussing and checking to make sure everything was in order, Dan and Ralph climbed aboard and started the engine. Hearing a sound like a blowtorch, Ralph suddenly leaped out of the boat into the water. There was fire in a carburetor. Fortunately the fire was pulled through the manifold and put itself out. Had it not, Dan soon would have joined Ralph for a swim. With the minor damage repaired, they drove *Miss Detroit* to speeds exceeding seventy miles an hour, an insane speed for a boat in those days. Ralph enjoyed it immensely, but, probably with some persuasion from his mother and his future wife, he sold the boat at the end of the summer. The next year he built a thirty-foot displacement boat named the *Siren*, powered with two six-cylinder engines. This project seems not to have been so successful; the extra power of the second engine was largely offset by its additional weight, but all future motorboats that Ralph owned he named *Siren*.

Ralph did not do all the manual labor on these boats himself. He employed a cabinetmaker, David Werking, and his cousin, Bert Teetor, a skilled toolmaker. Bert would assist Ralph with many of his projects in the future. But Ralph was always very much in charge, directing and checking every step, consulting, listening, knowing exactly how he thought each part should be installed. Many years later he gave the building where he worked on the boats to the Boy Scouts for a meeting place, but since that time, it has continued to be called "the Boat House" in memory of its prior use.

In 1921 Ralph persuaded his father and mother to purchase a cottage on the south shore of Lake Wawasee. During earlier visits to the area the family had stayed at the Sargent Hotel, but Ralph was arguing that facilities for keeping boats there were inadequate. No doubt he knew that his love affair with Chris and Jay Smith's beautiful mahogany boats would last a lifetime. The cottage that the Teetors bought had no heat, indoor plumbing, or electricity. But Ralph enjoyed fixing that kind of problem, and by the time he brought his bride there two years later it was much improved. He had the cottage wired for electricity, and he installed two bathrooms with modern plumbing. In the kitchen, however, he left a small pump at the edge of the sink; a larger pump stood just outside the back door. Adding to the charm of the place were the huge oak, walnut, and hickory trees which flourished along the lake's shoreline. They were so big one could be sure that many of them had shaded the Miami Indians who hunted and fished around the lake a hundred years before. It was an idyllic setting, and Ralph loved it.

Other Teetor cousins followed Ralph to Wawasee, renting, building, or purchasing summer cottages. Family played a key role in the social affairs of the summer here, as it did in Hagerstown.

Ralph and Nellie were en route to this favored destination the summer after they were married when, at a rain-slick intersection just north of Huntington, their car collided with another vehicle. A piece of shattered glass seriously cut Nellie's left eye. Fortunately, George and Louise Keagy were following in their car and immediately took Nellie to a doctor in Huntington, where she remained for several weeks. Naturally Ralph was terribly worried. At first, Nellie was told by the doctor that possibly she, too, would become blind; at best she would probably lose the sight in the injured eye. But her vision improved, and the other eye remained clear. Doctors then said she might see shadows but no more. However, her sight continued to improve, and in time, with glasses, she could see perfectly with both eyes. The doctors called it a miracle. Nellie simply replied, "I had to be able to see [for both of us]." For the rest of her life one could see faintly the line of the cut through the center of her left eye.

The days at the lake were carefree vacation getaways to be savored in small doses as frequently as possible throughout the hot summer. Most of the time, though, life in Hagerstown settled into a routine for the Teetor family. During these years Ralph usually walked the four blocks to the barbershop early each morning to be shaved. The barbershop was a social center as well as a grooming necessity. In the early 1920s before he and Nellie had their own home, he typically included a visit to Luther Parson's restaurant for breakfast, arriving about six o'clock to eat toast and cereal. No matter what his day's plans included, he always wore a clean white shirt, dark pants and tie, and, even at that early hour, he was jovial and friendly.

One summer morning Luther heard a racket outside his shop. Ralph walked into the restaurant looking dirty and disheveled, with several cobwebs clinging to his clothes and hair. With his normally cheerful demeanor gone and obviously in a frump, he sat on his usual stool at the end of the counter and ate his breakfast in silence. When he had finished he said, "Luther, someone left your cellar door open this morning and I fell into it." The cellar steps extended into the sidewalk and the door, when closed, formed part of that sidewalk. The cola delivery man had indeed neglected to close the door earlier that morning. Luther made sure that the delivery man was impressed with the importance of closing the door in the future.

Harold Rowe, who later became a factory associate, described the way Ralph found his way to the factory each day. Ralph walked past a hedge just before he turned to the door of the shop. He was accustomed to letting his hand brush lightly along the hedge to the end of the bushes from which he knew the number of steps to the office door. Ralph always walked purposefully and rapidly, never hesitating.

One day he missed the door, slamming his head into the wall beside it. The day before, the hedge had been trimmed back several inches, which caused Ralph's miscalculation. Such injuries were not unusual to this man who refused to compromise with a handicap. Much of the time Ralph carried a cut on his eyebrow from hitting a door or miscalculating a distance. He never complained. Apparently he considered it a small price to pay for his independence.


The summer of 1921 Ralph was appointed to the Hagerstown-Jefferson Township school board. The three members of the school board were the president and the treasurer, appointed by the town board, and the township trustee who served as secretary. Ralph served as president for seven years in a time which saw many changes in education in Hagerstown. When he joined the board in 1921, all twelve grades were still meeting in the same building he had attended twenty years before. The school was bulging; consolidation had added students from nearby villages which were closing most of the one-room schools in the area. According to school board minutes, five school "hacks" transported the children from the surrounding country. Each driver was paid seven dollars a day and expected to furnish the bus, install a "good heater," and pay all expenses.

School board minutes show that in early 1922 the board sold ninety thousand dollars in bonds to build a new, modern high school which was planned to house grades seven through twelve. Ralph loved to plan and build buildings, and the other members of the board deferred to him in many decisions, certainly all those concerning mechanical equipment. When a salesman displayed a piece of equipment that he was trying to sell the group, Ralph ran his hands all over it. After asking a few questions he usually had a much better understanding of how the item worked than anyone else on the committee. Because Ralph never compromised on quality, the new school had the latest and usually the best of everything.

The record of the school board during Ralph Teetor's service reflects the changes society was beginning to undergo in the twenties and the board's attempt to react to those changes. In 1926 the board went on record as opposed to "the employment of other married ladies as teachers in our schools." Early in 1928 the board held heated discussions on the new Teacher's Tenure law. The only split vote in seven years was recorded when the board members voted two-to-one that they would operate under the law. At the next meeting Ralph Teetor submitted his resignation as a school board member because "he was opposed to operating under the Teacher's Tenure Law." Tenure violated his standards of employee accountability. Ralph feared that tenure would encourage mediocrity and laziness, damaging the students' opportunity to get a good education. He predicted that good teachers didn't need the law and poor teachers could hide behind it. When he left he had served almost eight years, with his only absence being the day he was married.

The school board was only the first of several service obligations Ralph undertook to improve the education of young people. One of the most important to him was serving the Boy Scouts. There had been no Scout troop in Hagerstown when Ralph was a boy, the first one having been organized in 1912, the summer after Ralph graduated from college. Ralph encouraged Boy Scout competitions such as building and flying model airplanes and shooting archery by giving prizes to the winners. A boy who later would play a key role in Ralph's life told of winning a Scout uniform by building a little boat from a piece of wood, with nothing but a draw knife and a pocket knife. He attached a propeller powered with a rubber band stretched to a nail on the bow. Woody Ulrich related, "That little boat only worked well one time, the day it raced to first place for the uniform, which I wouldn't have had otherwise because we just couldn't afford to buy one at the time." Many years later Woody would become a key member of Ralph's most important engineering team at the Perfect Circle Corporation.

The Boy Scouts had no place to camp near Hagerstown, so Ralph bought a tract of twenty-eight acres about a mile south of the factory. This land contained the pond, now nearly dry, where, forty years before, ice had been harvested and stored for the summer. It also contained an old mill which one of Ralph's uncles, Lewis Teetor, had owned and operated before he became a Brethren minister. Ralph rebuilt the dam on the mill race to recreate the lake, built and wired for electricity a mess hall on the banks of the lake and officially gave the camp to the Scouts in the summer of 1928. The boys named it Camp Wapakamiki. Several years later the boys secured a larger campsite and Ralph then gave Wapakamiki to the Girl Scouts. Ralph continued his interest and support of Scouting for both boys and girls, serving local and regional councils, and was awarded the coveted Silver Beaver award for service to Scouting in 1931.

Nellie, too, actively supported Girl Scouting as her daughter participated. Later Nellie was elected president of the county-wide Girl Scout Council. On one occasion, after attending a camp recruitment meeting, she discovered that camping applications were not being given to the black girls. Quietly reprimanding those in charge of the recruitment, she let them know that any kind of discrimination would not be tolerated again in eastern Indiana. Girl Scout camp was for *all* girls. Although it was still many years before the Civil Rights movement would rise to fight such unkind treatment, Nellie simply saw each girl as a precious responsibility.


In 1920 the piston ring company was a quarter century old and, with little trouble, the directors had been able to carry out their policy of hiring all family members, including in-laws, who wanted a job. Fortunately, although these relatives were numerous, their gifts were both diverse and usually creative, so each one, if he chose, could find a niche where he could contribute successfully. Because of his failing health, John had taken little part in the daily activities of the factory, but he remained a close confidante and advisor to Charlie and, thus, a full participant in the decision-making for the company.

The 1920s saw the gradual transition from one generation to the next in the management of the family business. Like most generational transitions it was not completely smooth. The younger generation consisted of Ralph, George Keagy, Blair Hartley, and Charlie Teetor's four sons: Lothair, Macy, Don, and Herman. Charlie's brothers, Frank, Henry, and Joe Teetor had no sons.

There were marked generational differences. The older generation had scarcely attained a fifth-grade education while the younger men were all college graduates. The "seniors" had known very hard times indeed; the younger ones had grown up with opportunities, luxuries, and summer cottages. The older generation had built a decidedly successful company through sweat and long, long hours, and they were proud of their achievements. Some of the young ones had taken business courses and were full of theoretical knowledge. They were coming into a company where the structure was informal, and the lines of authority overlapping. The entire work-force still broke for lemonade and watermelon when the bosses felt like it. Still, the system had worked well while the company was small. No doubt the elders were uncomfortable with the changes which these "youngsters" with their book-learned business theories proposed. The potential for conflict was unavoidable.

Although Ralph and his cousins had been constantly on the spot at the factory most of their childhood, Ralph, as the oldest of his generation, was the first to seek official employment. Ralph, of course, had been working there since 1912, but he did not appear threatening to the senior generation. After all, he had learned all of his considerable mechanical skills from these masters. While Ralph had the theoretical training of the university, he and Charlie were on such a congruent mind track that even on the rare occasions when they disagreed, they respected each other. Now, with the title of Assistant Engineer, he worked with Charlie and others who were concerned with engineering or design problems. He also visited suppliers and automotive customers, providing a technical link to solve customer problems and assure quality products. Ralph was the first to recognize the importance of cooling cylinders. He helped auto company engineers find new ways to lubricate their engines and developed new methods to ensure piston rings would maintain a uniform pressure around the circumference of the piston. He was a favorite consultant for race car builders. Ralph's familiarity with the design and production of practically every part of the automobile engine gave him first-hand knowledge in diagnosing and solving problems.

Moreover, Charlie discovered soon after Ralph joined the company that he was able to build unusual relationships with customers and vendors by quickly gaining the respect and ear of presidents, chief engineers, and purchasing agents. Charlie frequently sent Ralph out to procure parts or solve some mechanical problem for a customer. This cheerful young blind man could visualize the mechanical processes of company engines so vividly that he could articulate and propose solutions to *their* engineering problems. He was sure of a warm reception wherever he went.

The result of this "skill" or "luck" was shown in his first meeting with Charles Kettering. Ralph related the story at the request of the Kettering Archives at General Motors in 1971.

*It was my good fortune to meet Mr. Kettering during 1914 when he was manufacturing starting, lighting and ignition equipment for automobile engines in his Delco plant in Dayton. I had graduated from college in 1912* and had joined our company doing engineering work. At this time our engines were all started with a hand crank on the front of the car, as the engines in most of the other cars were. By 1914 the Delco Company was supplying starting equipment for several of the popular automobile companies, so it was becoming necessary for us to equip the engines for our customers with electric starters.

It became my job to obtain and fit starters on our engines. I accordingly made an appointment with Mr. O. Lee Harrison, manager of Delco Company, and went to Dayton to contract with him to supply us with starters. After discussing our needs with Mr. Harrison, he explained to me that he was very sorry, but they had contracted to supply several larger automobile companies with their starting equipment, and that he was sure they would be unable to supply us with starters for a considerable time. I, of course, told him of our very urgent need for starters, but he regretfully told me that he could make no promises as to when they could deliver any equipment to us.

At about that moment the door of his office opened and the gentleman who appeared said to Mr. Harrison, "O. Lee, would you call me as soon as you have an opportunity?" Mr. Harrison said he would, and the door closed. Mr. Harrison asked me, "Do you know who that gentleman is?" and I answered, "No." "That was Mr. Charles Kettering," he said. "You probably know that he is the inventor of the electric starter." I replied, "Oh, yes!" and said that I knew of his accomplishments.

"Would you like to meet him?" asked Mr. Harrison. I, of course, said that I would like very much to meet him, so Mr. Harrison called Mr. Kettering into his office and introduced us.

I, naturally, very promptly told Mr. Kettering of the reason for my visit to their plant, and how badly we needed the starters for our engines, but that Mr. Harrison had just told me that they were not able to produce enough to supply our needs in addition to the equipment they had already promised. I must have impressed Mr. Kettering with our urgent need, for he immediately said to Mr. Harrison, "O. Lee, these people must have starters," and he assured me that they would take care of our requirements rather promptly.

Within thirty minutes we were ushered into Delco's engineering department where we designed brackets and fittings to mount the starters on *our engines. They were able to supply us with as much electric equipment as we needed very promptly, and we purchased Delco equipment for the following four years until we discontinued building complete automobile engines*

Based on a companionship formed of the mutuality of interest and temperament, the friendship between Ralph and Charles Kettering which began that day lasted all their lives. It was composed of small moments as well as large. Ralph liked to tell the story of a time when they met at breakfast at the Book Cadillac Hotel in Detroit. It was May 22, 1927, and Mrs. Kettering was reading the newspaper account of Charles Lindbergh's trans-Atlantic flight, which had been triumphantly completed from New York to Paris the day before.

"Wasn't it wonderful that he accomplished that, and to think that he did it all alone!" Mrs. Kettering exclaimed.

"Well, he could do it better alone than he could with a committee," Mr. Kettering snorted. It was typical of the wit and humor which Kettering's friends so well remembered.

Ralph's first years at the factory included traveling to the automobile companies which were, by this time, mostly situated in Detroit, selling the improved piston rings he was helping Charlie develop at home. Ralph was unique, the eldest of the new generation and himself an engineer, someone the older generation could understand. His uncles had taught him all they knew of fine craftsmanship and mechanical design, so now they could enjoy a sense of satisfaction in his success. He seemed to have spanned the generation gap with relative ease.

George Keagy had been the next of the "young ones" to appear at the factory for a job. A first cousin of Ralph's—his mother was a sister of Charlie and John's—he too had played at the factory from the time he could remember. George and Ralph had always been close friends. George had lived with Ralph at least two years while both were students at the University of Pennsylvania, and George graduated soon after Ralph with a degree in architecture. Back in Hagerstown he settled in as production manager at the plant, a position his father had held before him. Although this job took little advantage of his artistic talent, George accepted his new job with easygoing affability, so it appeared that he, too, slipped in fairly smoothly.

Blair, Charles Hartley's son, came to the factory in 1915 after graduating from the University of Wisconsin. A patient, kind, gentle man who could offend no one, Blair, too, blended into the company purchasing management with ease.

In 1921 Charlie's eldest son, Lothair Teetor, joined Indiana Piston Ring Company, and the next year Macy, his second son, arrived. Their assimilation into the company was not quite so smooth. Both Lothair and Macy were intelligent and highly talented, though their talents did not lie precisely in the engineering field. Lothair was a fine cornetist and during his Navy days had been invited by John Philip Sousa to join his band when the war ended. Macy had mastered the cornet, piano and organ and in college played in a dance orchestra led by fellow student Fred Waring. After graduation he arranged music and played piano for Waring until he returned to Hagerstown. While working as an engineer for the company, he still continued to play and compose as a hobby. Two of his songs became popular hits. Johnny Mercer wrote lyrics to Macy's tune "Lost"—a song which set a record in remaining at the top of the Hit Parade for thirteen weeks. The second, "I Saw You First," with words by Mack Davis, also enjoyed several weeks on the Hit Parade late in 1940. Both men would have preferred to pursue a career in music and might well have been successful. Their parents Charlie and Leora, however, did not consider music a proper vocation. Charlie wanted his sons to work at the company and his grandchildren to live nearby, so the young men really had no choice. Soon after their discharge from the Navy they were called back to Hagerstown.

Under such circumstances, with these young men feeling somewhat forced to join the company, the next few years were a test of family relationships and generational conflict, not an unusual occurrence in a family-held business. Lothair became sales manager, assuming the company's first full-time sales position; his sales philosophy presented an immediate problem.

The older generation, and Ralph along with them, believed that a company producing a desirable product at a reasonable price merely had to make the product available and people would buy their "better mousetrap." Lothair and Macy reflected the new age of advertising which designed specific campaigns for such products as Lucky Strike and Jell-O. They proposed that a good marketing program was as important as engineering and development. This presented an inevitable conflict of priorities, especially when the company had to allocate money to sales, advertising and engineering. Still, these disagreements were never aired beyond the boardroom or the family.

Underlying it all was a somewhat justifiable undercurrent of jealousy of the "fair-haired" cousin. Not only had Ralph been the first of his generation to be trained by his father and uncles in what they loved most to do, but he also showed exceptional talent and creativity in mechanical skills. Although Charlie's own sons were probably just as exceptional in other skills such as music, they could not compete with Ralph in engineering. Then too, Ralph's remarkable accomplishments "in spite of his blindness" elicited adulation and praise which would have been hard for any close associate to accept.

Certainly, too, Ralph's strong opinions and unyielding principles prevented easy compromise. All of these relatives worked in a business environment that was sometimes tense with disagreement. However, outside of the business no one would have suspected. The Teetor families supported each other, entertained each other, sometimes traveled together, and cared deeply about each other, all the while maintaining their different life philosophies and values. It was an unwritten rule that no one would discuss family problems with outsiders. They were first of all a family.

After he had graduated from the University of Illinois, Charlie's third son Donald joined the company and took over the sales department. Lothair had discovered that he hated sales. Finally Herman, youngest of Charlie's clan, came aboard and was assigned to advertising. These men comprised the new generation of management which would be Ralph's business associates for nearly forty years. One might assume, with their different ages and abilities, that salary expectations could create problems. Remarkably, they did not. The process they established first called for all the officers to agree on the total amount to be allocated to management salaries. Then each officer listed what he thought each person's salary ought to be, including his own, to reach the agreed-upon total figure. All lists were given to the secretary, who averaged them and assigned salaries. It seemed to have worked well for them, and no one later remembered any complaints.

The changes in the company and the potpourri of personalities inevitably became too much for several of the older generation. Joe and Henry Teetor retired in 1926. Joe returned to blacksmithing, which he loved, and Henry bought the cycle car business for one dollar and continued to manufacture the little cars. The world's huge appetite for these cars had been nearly satisfied, but repair and replacements provided a comfortable income for Henry's small shop. Two years later John, who had served as president of the family business thirty-two years, also stepped down. Charlie, known as "Dad" Teetor far beyond the family, assumed the presidency and occupied the office until he died in 1937.

The company grew rapidly through the twenties, riding the wave of the growing popularity of the automobile. The Model T, introduced in 1908, launched the opportunity for millions of people to participate in the miracle of auto transportation. The automobile was no longer just a Sunday afternoon entertainment—it was fast becoming an important means of "getting there." It needed paved roads, of course, to run on. Hagerstown paved its streets to the factory doors in 1919.

Now cars were driven more frequently by people other than the mechanics who could rebuild them, and they needed repair and replacement parts. Thus a new service industry was born—repair shops—and with them, a new market for piston rings. After ten to fifteen thousand miles of use, piston rings became worn. The worn rings needed to be replaced or the engine would burn oil. Since every engine model required a slightly different-sized piston ring, keeping these small shops supplied with all the sizes they might need seemed a formidable task. The credit for solving this dilemma must go to Lothair, who established a network of jobbers around the country to quickly provide every little crossroads repair shop with rings as they were needed—"just in time" delivery in 1921!

Strange as it sounds to us now, among some of the automobile manufacturers there was a considerable undercurrent of criticism and concern that the growing repair business would reduce future sales of new cars. Wouldn't automobile owners repair their old cars instead of buying new ones? The Teetors assured their automotive customers that the repair business would increase new car sales as well as bring new piston ring business and create more jobs. Of course time proved the Teetors correct, and the automobile companies eventually forgot their concerns.

The name Indiana Piston Ring Company was neither catchy nor memorable. To attract the new market of repair shop customers, the advertising department needed a good trade name. It was probably Hal Keeling, advertising specialist, who suggested that they call the piston rings *"Perfect Circles."* Ralph didn't care for that name at all, pointing out that if a circle isn't perfect, it isn't a circle. In addition, he said, until it was installed the piston ring wasn't really a circle at all because the cut in each ring permitted it to spring-fit inside the cylinder wall. If he had another name preference it is long forgotten. Perfect Circle it was to be. With the national advertising that followed, the Perfect Circle name became so well known that it was made the company name in 1926. Still, no matter how famous and respected the name became, it never quite won Ralph's approval. A circle had to be perfect or it wasn't a circle. Ralph devoted many years of work to ensuring that his circles were perfect.

Working with engines in boats and cars through the Teetor-Hartley Motor phase of the company, Ralph invented a fluid-actuated automatic gearshift. It was not the first automatic gearshift; a few of the very early cars had included automatic gearshifts using various principles, but none had proven long-lasting nor had been duplicated in later models. The drawings for Ralph's version of the auto-shift were finished in 1921 and a comprehensive patent was granted May 27, 1924. But he was doomed to disappointment: all his automotive manufacturing friends told him that people would not pay for the cost of such a luxury. What people have not tried, they rarely think they need, the thinking went. Finally Bendix Company bought the patent for twenty-five hundred dollars. Five years later Bendix supplied the

Hudson automobile with an automatic gearshift made from this patent. Enthusiasm for an automatic shift was slow to build during the Depression and World War II, but after the war its popularity exploded. By that time, of course, the patent had expired, but for the next forty years most of the automatic gearshifts on automobiles were made on the principles of Ralph's 1924 patent.

As the company grew, the stockholders prospered with it. Stockholders were not the only ones to benefit; almost everyone in town who wanted a job could find it at the piston ring company. Charlie liked it that way. He felt a strong responsibility to the folks of the little town to share his success as broadly as possible. By 1926 the company had employed nearly everyone Hagerstown could provide. It was time to find an expanded labor market for the company.

The company also needed a foundry. The men had developed a new method of casting piston rings individually in sand instead of the existing process of slicing them from a cylinder. In 1926, Perfect Circle purchased a building in New Castle, just eleven miles away, which was converted to a foundry. Now they had a reliable supply of castings and access to a new community of employees.

Abe Teetor and his son Dan were already making piston rings in Tipton, Indiana. Charlie had worked with his cousin Abe in a bicycle factory in Indianapolis back in the early 1890s. Abe and Ralph's father, John, were in the bicycle business together until John withdrew, soon after the Railway Inspection Car Company started. Abe had moved the bicycle business to a bigger building which burned down in 1905, but then he built a new company and began making parts for the booming automobile industry. By 1910 piston rings were Abe and Dan's specialty too. Now one of their accounts in particular was stretching their capacity. It had the foreign-sounding name of Chevrolet. Abe and Dan had just moved to a larger factory in Tipton, Indiana, when, in 1928, Charlie suggested that they merge the two piston ring companies. It was a good move. Dan, Ralph's childhood playmate and co-builder of the famous little car, brought his family to Hagerstown. He moved into the house just vacated by Ralph's parents, who had themselves just built a new, smaller home. Dan and Ralph resumed the close friendship they had enjoyed as children, a friendship which lasted the rest of their lives.

Even though Perfect Circle was a small company in a small town where everyone knew each other on a first-name basis, this did not guarantee total harmony between managers and hourly workers. The first break came in February, 1929. At this time the men who ran the lathes were paid between forty and fifty cents an hour for ten-hour, six-day weeks. Management, deciding that wages should better reflect the quality of the job done, announced that in the future the men would be paid forty-five cents an hour for a standard number of pieces with an incentive for higher output. In addition, a change in accounting procedures would result in payday twice a month instead of every week. This looked like a pay cut to the employees, and on February seventh about one hundred of them struck, asking for cancellation of the changes. Ralph and Lothair headed a committee to solve the dilemma and bring peace.

Ralph, addressing the strikers two days later, was quoted in the local *Exponent* as saying he was hopeful that all of the men who walked out would return to the plant. He offered to receive them in a body if they returned the following Monday. He insisted, however, that the strikers give the new wage system a fair trial.

As the paper reported:

*"The new wage payment system might not be perfect at this time,"* Vice President Teetor stated, but he assured the men that if this fact was definitely established the plan would be modified to the satisfaction of the employees.

*"It is not the desire of the company that the wages of its employees be reduced,"* the blind executive announced. "As a matter of fact, the company wants its employees to receive larger wages, and to that end this new wage payment system has been inaugurated. If the plan is imperfect it will be rectified. We only ask that our employees have confidence in the company."*

At the conclusion of Mr. Teetor's brief remarks the strikers applauded him vigorously.

The strikers did not come back on Monday but straggled in soon after. The new wage system did prove to be acceptable and nothing more was heard about it.

Life in the company and in the town proceeded on an even keel. After all, it was the confident twenties and the mood of the country was buoyant and optimistic. Every day was sure to be better than the last.

To be sure, in this age of prosperity, disappointment and tragedy did not declare a moratorium, especially on a personal level. In 1927 Ralph and Nellie were expecting their first child. Near the end of the pregnancy, Nellie developed toxemia and their baby boy was born dead. Of course they would continue to try to have children. There was still plenty of time.

*Ralph Teetor, 1922.*

*Nellie as a young woman, 1922.*

*Nellie Van Antwerp at the age of five, 1899.*

*Nellie and Ralph in first Siren at Wawasee about the year 1918. It was the second boat built in Hagerstown, thirty feet long with two six-cylinder Teetor-Hartley motors. (Courtesy of Jack Teetor)*

*Patent for hydraulic gear shift for automobiles, 1924.*

Siren II — Ralph's first Chris Craft, twenty-two feet long, on Wawasee. Front seat: Fred Duesenberg, Ralph, Dan Teetor driving. (Courtesy of Jack Teetor)

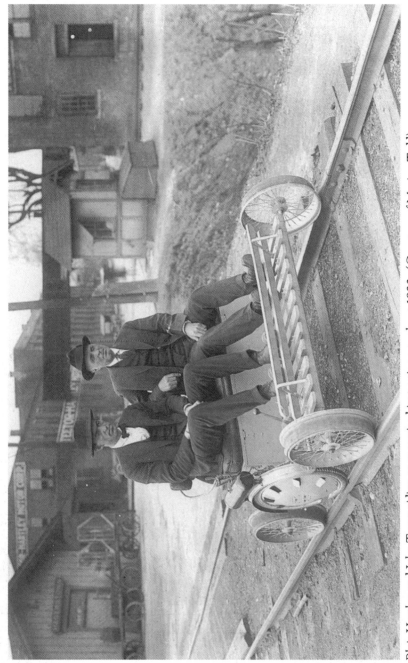

*Blair Hartley and John Teetor riding on motorized inspection car about 1920. (Courtesy of Marion Todd)*

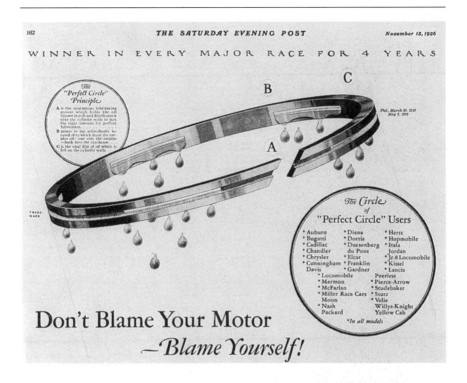

*Perfect Circle at some time around 1928.*

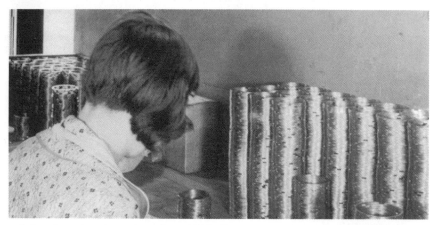

*Manufacturing piston rings about 1930. From pig iron to grinding to inspection. (Hagerstown Museum Collection)*

# The Not So Depressing 1930s

It was Black Tuesday on Wall Street, October 29, 1929, a day which turned the world of finance upside down. Ralph knew nothing of the crash until late in the evening; he had spent the day becoming a member of the Masonic Lodge. There was a satisfaction and certain taste of victory in his Masonic ritual; special dispensation had been obtained so Ralph, a blind man, could be granted membership.

A few days before this, Ralph had purchased one hundred shares of General Motors Corporation stock. Because he knew the management personally, he thought GM was an exceptionally good investment. As was the custom at that time when one purchased stock, he bought on 10 percent margin, although he had the cash to pay the rest and planned to do so when the broker sent him a bill. When the stock prices started falling on the day of the crash, brokers called their margin clients to "cover," or pay an amount equal to what the stock had lost. If the client did not "cover," the broker would repossess the stock to sell for whatever price he could get.

Ralph, spending the day at the Masonic Lodge, could not be reached by phone and so the broker sold. The next day Ralph learned that he had lost his one hundred shares of General Motors. The broker lost a disgruntled customer. Many years later Ralph would tell the story as a lesson in the careful use of credit. But he liked to estimate how many times that one hundred shares of General Motors had multiplied in value. As time went on the story got bigger and the value increased. However, practical Nellie always reminded him that he never would have kept the stock that long anyway. At any rate, the crash of 1929 was of little lasting concern to him because his original stake was small.

Perfect Circle became a public company in 1928. While it remained a tightly-held family business, the family stockholders could now realize some profit from the growth of their original investment. As a result, Ralph became very interested in the workings of the stock market, investing in companies which he respected and also which he thought would grow. During most of the early 1930s "yea-sayers" and sages convincingly predicted a recovery that was "just around the corner." At the time, no one had any idea how long it would take for the crash and its ensuing economic slump to play out. Ralph was patient.

Through those desert years of Depression, Hagerstown remained an oasis of prosperity, thanks to the now firmly entrenched popularity of the automobile. The automobile had by this time turned from a "rich man's toy" to a middle class expectation and a symbol of realizing the American Dream. The automobile in the thirties exemplified freedom, speed, mobility, autonomy, and power. It changed people's values, for owning a car had become as important to many as providing food, clothing and shelter. In fact, during this Depression one could find many people skimping on food and clothing to keep their Fords or Oldsmobiles running. While new car sales plummeted as the Depression deepened, car owners still kept the old ones repaired. As a result, during those struggling years piston ring sales to repair shops became Perfect Circle's dominant business. While this niche didn't compensate for all the new car business lost during the lean years, the replacement ring division enjoyed a high profit margin, and most of those years the company continued to grow. Perfect Circle's fortunate decision to advertise to the general public began to pay dividends too. In late 1930 the type "85" Oil-Regulating ring, continuing a series of significantly improved piston rings, carried Perfect Circle further and further ahead of their competition. Major piston ring improvements in 1933, 1935, and 1937 increased engine efficiency and reduced wear. The automotive market was growing and Perfect Circle's share within that market grew also; consequently the company poured more money and effort into research and development. Design improvement was, of course, under Ralph's leadership but neither he nor any of the engineers working with him were singled out for individual credit. They all stood tall together.

Some of the growth was due to the acuity of Perfect Circle's president Charlie Teetor. His sense of humanity was a strong part of his leadership. There were still a few people in town who worked for other industries. As the Depression deepened and these folks lost their jobs, they could count on employment at Perfect Circle. There were months when everyone's hours were cut back to as few as three ten-hour days per week, but no one was ever laid off in the thirties. One of the former employees who worked in the tool room remembered, "Sometimes we worked a week and then were off a week but everyone who needed a job had one." *The Circle* employee newsletter announced that they would no longer hire married women, only men and single women who were heads of households. It was management's obligation to give jobs to those who needed them most. In fact, employment grew from 825 in 1931 to 1,087 in 1933 and stayed close to that figure until World War II. It was Charlie's way and everyone took pride in it.

Company growth required more space, and in 1928 Perfect Circle began an extensive building program which more than doubled the capacity of the factory. It ended in 1934 when the new facilities were completed with a gala all-employee party with much joking and mirth in the new cafeteria.

During the 1920s and 1930s employee picnics in the summer, band concerts (Perfect Circle had an excellent band), and holiday parties, always enthusiastically attended by Charlie and Ralph, promoted a family spirit among employees. The greatest climax of all the Perfect Circle parties occurred in 1934 in Cleveland, Ohio, at the important automotive parts show. Perfect Circle threw a party for all its customers in the United States and overseas. The seven hundred guests enjoyed observing Lowell Thomas, the well known pioneer radio newscaster, broadcast his nightly newscast from the speaker's table, an electronic first. Following a six-course feast the guests were entertained by Phil Spitalney, a young Italian orchestra leader, still unknown beyond New York City, and his beautiful all-girl orchestra.

Lowell Thomas in his remarks said, "This is the banquet by which all future banquets should be judged." Gordon Murray, who arranged this event, estimated that Perfect Circle spent fifty-five dollars per person on the elegant gala, an unheard of cost for an evening in 1934. "Competitors were really *zapped* that evening while all their customers were at our party having a wonderful time," according to Murray.

Although the residents of Hagerstown were spared many of the ravages of the Depression, tramps became common, riding in on the trains and stopping for handouts before going on. They were decent men, just out of a job and down on their luck, hoping that the grass would be greener beyond some faraway fence. Several of the women in Hagerstown took pity on these men, keeping a pot of stew or soup on the stove to provide a nourishing meal when these transients came to the door. Nellie was among those compassionate women handing out a bowl of food to whoever asked. But as hard times dragged on, the word of her generosity spread and the parade of tramps to her back door increased. In the summer of 1934 the numbers grew rapidly—sixteen one day, eighteen the next, then twenty-two, twenty-four. Nellie knew she could not keep up her soup kitchen for so many. She finally had to say to the next ones who stopped, "No, I have nothing for you." Afterward, she cried.

But tears were an exception in the Ralph Teetor household—these were good years for this family. By fall of 1930, Nellie was again expecting a baby. With either rash confidence in a successful pregnancy (considering the former history) or a strong desire on Nellie's part to relieve her parents-in-law of their permanent summer guests at Lake Wawasee, she and Ralph purchased their own cottage at the lake, again right next door to Ralph's parents. It was a wonderful old rambling frame house right on the shore of the lake, first built in 1887, with major additions which had been made as the family of the previous owner had grown. What the cottage lacked in organization, it made up in character and size. As he loved to do, Ralph remodeled the house that winter, rearranging the living room and porch walls, adding bathrooms, furnace, kitchen, and other conveniences. Since the house was built just for a summer cottage with thin, wooden walls, remodeling was fairly simple, so he continued changing and improving this lake house through most of the next twenty-five years.

He loved to be at the lake, tinkering with the boats and motors. Still a loyal friend of Chris and Jay Smith, he owned nothing but Chris Craft motor boats, convinced that they were the best boats made. Much of the time he owned two different sizes. He rigged up a unique arrangement in the concrete boathouse in which one boat was lifted by a hoist several feet above the water, and the second one was stored floating underneath. Just a quarter horsepower electric motor ran the hoist, which slowly raised one boat on two cables hooked into eyes on the deck of the boat, and wrapped around a horizontal bar along the ceiling. To lower the boat, the same motor applied a brake to the unwinding cables, but could not stop the boat's descent once it began to lower. In fact, trying to stop the boat by turning the motor off merely removed the brake and the boat dropped faster. On more than one occasion a guest unfamiliar with this arrangement started the top boat down while the lower one remained in the well. There would be an embarrassing crash, usually resulting in minor damage. Ralph was never angry about this, always reassuring the remorseful friend or relative that it was his own fault because he hadn't told the guest how the hoist worked. Puttering around the boats, Ralph's personal radar and natural caution were not infallible. More than once he fell into the lake. With disgust for his carelessness, he worried more about his pocket watch than his clothes.

Ralph enjoyed fishing and occasionally cast his line into Lake Wawasee with friends. The mechanical precision of good fishing gear intrigued him. Since his mind never stopped focusing on ways to improve most anything, the fishing trips drew his attention to fishing poles. After a couple of hours sitting in the boat holding the pole handle over the water, he wondered why a fishing pole grip was always made in a line with the pole, tiring the wrist of the holder. Ralph thought that it would be much more comfortable to hold a pole if the handle was a pistol-grip like a gun.

Back on shore Ralph continued to think that his pistol-grip fishing pole handle was a distinct improvement over the conventional one. He contacted George Craig, a patent attorney. After searching for existing patents George told Ralph that there were three patents covering a variety of handles which, in Craig's opinion, prevented Ralph from obtaining a patent on his idea. The year was 1924.

Since he had just received the patent on his gearshift, Ralph did nothing more about his fishing pole handle until 1930. Then he must have experienced another quiet day of fishing. He designed a depression on the side of his pistol-shaped handle that would attach the reel in a more convenient place. By this time Perfect Circle had a different patent attorney, and Ralph asked the new man to prepare an application for a patent on the combination of the pistol grip and the improved method of attaching the reel. The same conflicting patents were still in force and his counsel, Harry Lindsey, gave him the same advice that Mr. Craig had given six years previously—you can't do it! The handle looked different from the others so a design patent could be obtained, but a mechanical patent would conflict with the previous claims. Ralph applied for a mechanical patent anyway but was rejected as Lindsey predicted.

The incident reveals a dogged persistence that marked Ralph's whole life and accounted for many of his achievements. This man, who had built and driven a car at age twelve and had graduated from college after being told he couldn't do it was not to be stopped so easily. He had models made from the other patents and then wrote the following, in part, to Harry Lindsey:

*We may possibly see each other within the next few days, but I thought in case we would not I might be able to give you some thoughts on the rejection. I think the patent office is all wet on their rejection of the various claims. In the first place, Hanson's scheme [one of the patents] is scarcely usable. In his design the reel sits so high above the handle that it could not be properly controlled by the thumb when casting or paying out line. I know this is true for the first one I made was of this type and so far as any fisherman is concerned it would be entirely worthless. It is only by a very carefully designing of the combination of the depression and the pistol grip that the scheme can be made practical.*

*It is true that Zass [another one of the conflicting patents] can use his depression with the straight handle as he does, but he does not show the combination of the pistol grip and the depression, which is the all-important thing. In view of this necessity I think the Examiner is wrong in his rejection of claim 6 in which they advise that the nut is the full equivalent of our thumbscrew with the conical end. It would be absolutely impossible to make Hanson's scheme of locking the reel practical in connection with the pistol grip he shows . . .*

Harry continued to be discouraging. They could possibly patent the device for attaching the reel to the pole, but a broad patent to cover the whole combination was very doubtful. However, the attorney was planning to be in Washington in about six weeks on another matter and, if Ralph still wished him to work on it he would see what he could accomplish.

Ralph immediately shot back:

*I just believe that if I took a handle with a reel mounted on it to the Patent Office I could explain to the Examiner the difference in the combination of the recessed reel and pistol grip handle. It might be possible that I could be in Washington with you. That is, however, quite a ways off and we will discuss the details later on.*

It is not known whether Ralph went to Washington to plead his case before the patent examiner. But six months later an application for his patent was filed, and the patent was granted one month after that, on February 21, 1933. It contained everything he wanted.

Ralph now turned his effort to the possibility of manufacturing and selling this wonderful fishing pole handle. He contacted potential suppliers for quotes on parts. He also visited James Heddon's Sons fishing tackle manufacturers to determine their interest in selling it. They weren't enthusiastic.

Typically he gave several of his friends one of the handles to try out. "This is good for still fishing" they agreed, "but it isn't so good for casting. You need a straight handle for that."

"What if we put in a hinge?" asked Ralph, still thinking there was room for improvement. On October 16, 1933, a new letter was sent off to Harry Lindsey:

*As usual, I have another idea which the enclosed print will describe. You will readily see that it is in connection with the Fishing Pole Handle.*

*This is a further improvement which, I believe, is patentable, and if you agree with me, I would like to prepare and file an application. I think the sketch is self-explanatory and will show the handle exactly the same as was specified in the other patent except where the handle portion joins the body of the device there is a hinge introduced. This hinge permits the angle between the handle and the main body portion to be varied from a straight or parallel line to approximately the same angle as was shown in the other patent. This offers considerable advantage due to the fact that many fishermen wish to use a straight handle for casting whereas they prefer to have it angled for trolling . . ..*

Six months later Ralph had a third patent on his fishing pole handle. The only evidence that he tried to sell this device is at the end of an article in *The Hagerstown Exponent.* After much praise for the patent and comfortable design of the fishing pole handle the newspaper informs, "Ralph is receiving sealed bids from scores of fishing rod manufacturers who are anxious to obtain manufacturing rights. 'If they have something besides script to pay with I might be induced to sell the patent,' Mr. Teetor said. Meanwhile, he is keeping the new device away from curious eyes." He was joking, of course; no one was beating down the door to buy the thing.

By this time Ralph was too busy with other activities to pursue the matter further. But he was tenacious—definitely. A brick wall would stop him, but only when he was convinced that the wall really was solid brick with no way around it. Many times he explored an idea, dropped it, and then picked it up again years later. He would be ready when he found a crack in the wall.

One of Ralph's adventures in the early thirties was a quick springtime trip to Daytona Beach, Florida, with his good friend and fellow inventor, Clessie Cummins. Clessie, like Ralph, had been inventing mechanical devices all his life. Early in the century Clessie had worked briefly for the Light Inspection Car Company as the piston ring business was developing. Now, financed by W. G. Irwin of Columbus, Indiana, Clessie was developing the product that would form the sales base for what would become the worldwide Cummins Engine Company.

Clessie's life's work was the diesel engine, first developed for boats, then for trains and automobiles, and later for trucks. The romance of the diesel engine is described very entertainingly in his book, *My Days with the Diesel*. According to Clessie's account, early in 1930 he had installed the first diesel engine in an automobile. Totally convinced that diesel-powered cars could develop into a major market, he needed to build his credibility in the automotive industry. One of the early methods of testing and promoting automobiles was racing them to achieve new speed records, especially on the smooth, hard sand of Daytona Beach. Learning that prominent speed driver Kaye Don, of Great Britain, planned to attempt a new speed record at Daytona, Clessie realized that the international press would be at the Florida city. He planned to catch their attention with a diesel speed record of his own. When the time came, mechanical problems delayed Don's speed attempt and the reporters converged on Clessie, giving him more publicity for his diesel than he had dared hope for.

Clessie had asked Ralph to accompany him to Florida, presumably because, in addition to being a friend, Ralph had a unique talent for diagnosing the condition of any engine by the sound it made. If anything was wrong, Ralph Teetor usually knew exactly what the mechanical difficulty was by listening to the engine. Many stories exist of Ralph's being the first to notice, or the first to figure out, the cause of an engine problem.

For Ralph, going to Daytona with his friend was a lark. It was usually great fun to be with the intelligent and amusing Clessie Cummins. And, of course, Ralph loved to be a part of what was new, faster, and possibly better, in automobiles and mechanics.

Early one summer evening of 1931 another of Ralph's automotive friends brought his creation to Ralph for approval and admiration. Fred Duesenberg is best remembered for his race cars at the Indianapolis Speedway, but his enthusiasms included fast boats and, of course, the automobile that bore his name. Fred and Ralph, longtime friends and kindred spirits, desired that whatever they built should be as perfect as they could make it, regardless of cost. Fred had just completed a prototype of his new Model SJ, the ultimate in power and beauty, and custom-built, as its advertising claimed, "to outclass, outrun, and outlast any car on the road." Leaving Indianapolis after work, Fred drove the sixty miles to Hagerstown to show Ralph the new supercharged model which he intended to have ready for the market the next year. Anticipating his arrival, Ralph called Dan, then living across the street, who brought his eight-year-old son Jack to see the new model. When Fred arrived, everyone piled into the big car with Dan driving, Ralph beside him with little Jack on his lap, and Fred in the back seat. Besides the size and power of that awesome machine, Jack today remembers the impressive instrument panel. In addition to the conventional gas gauge, oil pressure gauge, engine heat indicator, and ammeter to measure battery charge, there was a 150-MPH speedometer, a 5,000-RPM tachometer, an altimeter to measure altitude above sea level, and an eight-day clock with split-second hand. Lights glowed to advise the driver to change the oil and to check the water in the battery at appropriate times.

Since Fred Duesenberg's first love was racing, the dazzling array of polished metal and the glistening green enameled engine beneath the hood was the finest that mechanical genius could produce. This supercharged giant developed 320 horsepower; the catalog claimed the big car could go 129 MPH in top gear and 104 MPH in second. It was capable of accelerating from 0 to 100 MPH in seventeen seconds. Dan, a cautious driver even then, would not have dared to come close to testing the car's limits, but still it was an exciting experience for two car buffs and a little boy.

Fred still had one more feature of the SJ to show Ralph—its speed. Shortly after the evening in Hagerstown, they met at the Indianapolis Speedway "to see what it would do." They "did" in excess of one hundred miles an hour. Many years later Ralph commented that it was an experience he did not care to repeat.

Unfortunately, the cost of this luxury cruiser was to contribute to the demise of the Duesenberg Motor Company and later the Auburn Motor Company which bought Duesenberg. This sad failure was the fate of the few remaining automobile companies which produced hand-crafted, expensive automobiles for a dwindling supply of wealthy customers during those prolonged Depression years. Still the Duesenberg was a classic, one of many important contributors to the development of the automotive industry and to American cultural history.

Ralph, Clessie, Fred, and other automotive pioneers knew that they were making history, that the world would never be the same now that the remarkable machines they were helping to manufacture were achieving widespread popularity. Drawn together by a shared vision of a better life, they rejoiced in each other's successes. When they failed, they considered the failure part of the process—they just had to "work a little longer."

As Ralph became well known for his unique skill in engineering and improving automobiles, he developed close relationships with the officers and engineers of nearly all the automotive companies of the time such as Jim Zeder, Chrysler Corporation; Charles Kettering, General Motors Corporation; Ed Cole, Studebaker Corporation (later, General Motors); Arch Calwell, Thompson Products; Jim Crawford, Chevrolet; Arthur Nutt, Packard Motor Car Company; and Art Rosen, Caterpillar Tractor Company. This professional collegiality was enhanced through membership in the Society of Automotive Engineers, an association which Ralph was finding increasingly important. When founded as a technical society in 1905, SAE offered sociability in addition to the sharing of technical information to those few pioneers who were starting an industry. It was still small when Ralph joined in 1911 while he was a college student. World War I marked a milestone—SAE mobilized its engineering talent to develop power plants for Navy submarines and aircraft. While Ralph was not directly involved in this undertaking, shortly after he returned from the shipyards of Philadelphia, he became active in the technical committees of the society. In 1927 he was elected chairman of the Indiana Section, and then became president of SAE in 1936. The position required him to make an extensive speaking tour across the United States. News reports from that tour leave us with one record of Ralph's enthusiasm and vision for the automobile industry at that time:

*We have gone just about as far as it is practical to go in building for power and speed, but there remain two important fields for progress, economy and safety . . .*

*The cheaper production of automobiles is inevitable as the industry retains its youth, its zest for battle in keen competition. The history of the industry, from year to year, has been giving more for less money, and that tendency will be accelerated . . .*

*The solution may be the diesel engine, but that is not certain. We are sure only of the fact that the cost of running an automobile will be surprisingly less in the future . . .*

*The automotive industry is greatly interested in the crusade to lower traffic accidents. The principle way to reduce accidents is to teach careful driving. We should teach drivers to observe the rules. But this doesn't seem to be easy. The chief problem in this entire matter is to get people to respect the rules of driving. This can't be done with mechanics; it must be done by thinking, by observation upon the part of drivers.*

*Another thing, highways should be improved; curves should be smoothed out, overhead crossings built over railroad lines and avenues for fast traffic, taking out dangerous sections of road and widening many of them.*

*The industry can, if it will, voluntarily solve the problem of traffic accidents. If, however, the industry is unwilling to recognize its obligations in this respect, it must then face the fact that it will be subjected to discipline from other sources.*

The presidency of SAE brought Ralph recognition in engineering circles both in the United States and in Europe, even a picture and article in *Time* magazine. He continued to be a popular speaker at engineering meetings. At the beginning of World War II, SAE, remembering the valuable contribution it offered during the first World War, formed a committee of eighteen leading engineers from diverse fields of experience to solve the equipment problems of the armed forces. As a member of this committee, Ralph was again in the forefront of research, his particular challenge being to increase the life of the pistons in the tank and aircraft engines which had to operate in north African deserts. But that is ahead of the story.

It wasn't just in the professional world that Ralph noted milestones in the 1930s. In April, 1931, Nellie gave birth to a daughter. I would be their only child and they honestly gave me every advantage within their power. Just as they expected excellence in every other area of their lives, both Nellie and Ralph threw their full energies into being superlative parents. Doting on every breath their baby daughter took, they were particularly shaken when, a year later, Charles Lindbergh's baby, the same age as their Marjorie, was kidnapped and killed. They, along with the entire country, so identified with the distraught parents that it shadowed much of their enjoyment for some time. It even influenced the design for the new house that was now being planned.

For several years Ralph had been purchasing land at the edge of Hagerstown on which to build his dream home; he had given a good deal of thought to just how it should be designed. He wanted this house to serve more than one purpose. Because Hagerstown was distant from any large city, there was no hotel appropriate for Perfect Circle's corporate guests. They would be guests in this gracious home. By 1931 Ralph had put together a number of pieces of pasture, hillside and floodplain that totaled nearly thirty acres. He was ready to begin. The house would look out over a broad meadow bounded by a tiny stream. In the distance the family could see an old mill and a railroad track from whose boundaries would reverberate the wails of train whistles and the soft chugging of locomotives. A bit nearer stood the English Tudor home of Charlie Teetor, built thirty years before.

The next year Ralph and Nellie met with architects Pierre and Wright to put their dreams into blueprint form. The plans went through many changes, and on each new set of blueprints which the architects prepared, they glued narrow strips of paper along the outlines of the rooms. Ralph could then follow with his fingers exactly where rooms, doors, windows, stairs—everything—would be. He enjoyed explaining the plans to others, running his fingers around these little ridges, pointing to the rooms and doors. With his excellent memory for dimensions, he was able to give his audience a complete tour of the proposed house.

Farmland was still being cleared in eastern Indiana and, at Ralph's request, for many years sawmill owner Earl Whipple had been saving choice boards of wild cherry for paneling. That cherry eventually paneled the large entrance hall, the staircase, upper hall, and much of the living room with its Steinway grand piano. The piano contained an electric Duo Art player which reproduced the notes and expression found on three hundred or so rolls kept in a cupboard behind the piano. Ralph loved to listen to the music and memorized the position in the cupboard of his favorite pieces, enabling him to select them unaided. He also enjoyed astounding his friends by asking them what they wished to hear and then pulling out a Beethoven or Rachmaninoff as if he could read the labels. The mechanical precision, beautiful music and flair for showmanship of the Duo Art reproducer ensured Ralph's enthusiasm.

The stairs drew Ralph's special attention. His business travel frequently took him to New York, where he usually stayed at the Waldorf Astoria Hotel. As he walked into that hotel from the street and climbed a grand stairway to the lobby, he noticed that the climb did not tire him as much as did other flights of stairs. He learned that architects had discovered that a properly proportioned stairway required the least amount of energy to climb. These ideal dimensions consist of an eleven-inch tread and a six-and-a-half inch riser—neither too steep nor too gradual. The grand staircase in his new house, then, had to be made of exactly these dimensions. However, no one ever saw him climb any of those stairs fewer than two, sometimes three, at a time before he reached the age of seventy-five.

Behind the staircase was a very large, leaded-paned window, imbedded with five stained-glass, medallion-like pictures of ethereal ladies symbolizing the four seasons, so typical of the art deco style of the 1930s.

True to Ralph's abiding interests, this house was planned to include the latest in building technology, over two miles of wiring, full house air-conditioning and an elaborate speaker system for radio and chimes everywhere. The radio was Ralph's newspaper as well as occasional entertainment. He built a fine radio and record player into a library closet and wired them to individually controlled speakers in five other rooms including his workshop. Telephones, doorbells, and several clocks chimed, each with its own unique tone, sometimes disconcertingly to guests. In a day when a significant percentage of his neighbors were still using outhouses, the four family and guest bedrooms each had its own tiled bath. Ralph's shower in the master bathroom contained ten shower heads, one in the conventional place overhead and three vertically along each wall. With memories of the Lindbergh kidnapping in mind, Ralph and Nellie planned for the two connecting family bedrooms to be locked off from the rest of the house if desired.

Fellow engineers were amazed at the fully equipped machine shop in the basement with the latest model lathe, milling machine, drill press, and grinder. Special footings were poured for these heavy machines, some of which had to be installed as the house was being built, because they were too big to move through the doors.

To build the house, my father turned to a young contractor from Indianapolis, Carl Geupel. Although Geupel had built many of the new buildings at Perfect Circle and had supervised construction on banks and commercial buildings, he had never built a house. That was fine with Ralph; Geupel's commercial expertise would stand him in good stead for the standards Ralph wished to maintain. The house would be built like a bank—poured concrete over reinforcing steel for all the floors and walls. Elmer Wilson, a carpenter who helped build the house, related that his crew had a hard time getting the studding in because every evening when Ralph came to the house to look over what had been done that day, he would usually change it. Most people might think that moving a door or window two or three inches to one side might not matter, but to Ralph it was important; all must be perfect. Finally the carpenters just tacked in their new work each day so they could more easily comply with Ralph's changes. Ralph's feet were as sensitive as his hands. If floors or steps were not perfectly level, Ralph knew by merely walking on them, and they were rebuilt. When the house was finished three years later, it was exactly as Ralph and Nellie wanted it.

Ten acres of lawn, many trees and a large house required help for Ralph and Nellie to maintain. One of the people they hired was Shib, a short Japanese man of about thirty who had come to the United States probably to escape an arranged marriage. Previously, Shib had worked for the Stoughton Fletchers in Indianapolis for many years. He was hired to plant flowers and vegetables as well as clean the house. Nellie soon discovered that he was also skilled in elegant ways of presenting and serving food, a skill commonly taught in Japan. Although he lived in a room in town, he adopted the Teetor family as his own; and to a large extent, the Ralph Teetor family adopted him. He taught me many Japanese words.

In the spring of 1937 the rains came, and the Ohio River went on a rampage, overflowing its banks and creating havoc in southern Ohio and Indiana. A call went out for boats to help rescue hundreds of people stranded on their rooftops. Without hesitation Ralph called on Horace Marlatt, his chauffeur, to take his Chris Craft on a trailer from Wawasee to Cincinnati, where it was launched to spend several days on its mission of mercy. By the time Horace and *Siren III* got to the flood, the crisis was about over and Horace reported that the trip was mostly a waste of time. But to me, a little girl of six, it seemed dramatically heroic.

The same rains that swelled the Ohio flooded the streams in eastern Indiana, although with less disastrous consequences. The little creek flowing through the meadow in front of the new house also overflowed its banks, causing water to run disturbingly close to the house. Ralph resolved to "fix" that. To prevent a reoccurrence of the threat of a flood, he would "straighten the creek."

After the water receded, it took men working with large earth-moving equipment several months to accomplish what Ralph had in mind. He went out each day to check the work. After the crew had finished un-kinking the creek, for good measure Ralph had them build a six-foot-high levee along one side of the meadow. This undertaking necessitated running the creek through a large viaduct under the levee. There were some folks in Hagerstown who judged this to be more elaborate than necessary, but Ralph never planned to fix anything twice. The most severe test of the system since that time came in

1993 when a cloudburst caused serious local flooding. The water rose to the top of the levee and finally spilled over it for the first time in all those years. But that incident also proved that the levee had been so precisely engineered that it controlled the flood waters to prevent damage both above the levee and below. After fifty-six years it worked exactly as it had been planned.

As the Depression deepened in 1931 and 1932, the country became impatient and discouraged with the perceived "do-nothing" solutions of President Herbert Hoover and turned to Franklin D. Roosevelt with his promises of a New Deal. The Teetor family, traditionally Republican anyway, was opposed to New Deal programs from the beginning in 1933. Above all they sensed that the New Deal was unrealistically raising the expectations of people through the government's redistribution of wealth. As they saw it, with relief laws being passed people learned they could get something for doing nothing and did not have to work hard to earn what they desired. Having had to make his own way in a doubting world, Ralph was outspoken about the perils of this "New Deal." Ralph's cousin Lothair agreed with Ralph. Lothair carried out his conservative convictions by becoming active in public affairs, eventually serving as Assistant Secretary of Commerce in the Eisenhower administration. Ralph bought books about economics and the value of hard work to distribute among his friends, wrote letters, and through his wide circle of acquaintances, and promoted his economic and political opinions. He took advantage of every opportunity to deepen public understanding of the importance of freedom, competition, and self reliance in the history of the nation and the contributions of industry to the public good.

He took to the political soapbox in this article written for *The Circle* employee newsletter:

### What it Costs to Create and Maintain a Perfect Circle Job

*All business starts with an investment of capital. Someone saves some money. He rents a building, buys some machinery and supplies, employs some people and starts to make and sell a product. Or, the man who saved* his money may wish to start a store; in which case, he buys store equipment and merchandise, employs salespeople and becomes a merchant. Or, he may wish to own a part of a business and take no part in the management; in which case, he pays his money to the management of a business and receives in return a stock certificate showing that he owns a certain part of that business.

Perfect Circle stockholders are of two kinds. Those who take an active part in the management and those who buy Perfect Circle stock as an investment; but in each case, money that was saved was invested in this business creating it in the first place and causing the business to grow.

The first investment of capital in a few machines created jobs for just a few men. Then, as more and more capital was added to the business, more machines and men were needed.

Few of us realize as we come to work in the morning the investment of capital required to make a job for us. We, of course, know that it takes buildings that are heated and lighted, that it takes machinery to produce our products, and raw material or castings upon which to work. But there is actually almost as much capital invested which we cannot see as in the tangible things we see each day.

A look at the figures in terms of what is invested for each individual employee is interesting. Here is the investment needed to support the average Perfect Circle employee today (1937):

| Investment | | Per Employee |
|---|---|---|
| Working Capital..........$1,088,094 | ................. | $977 |
| Cash Outstanding for Mdse. Sold ...........400,857 | ................... | 364 |
| Inventory of Raw/ Finished Products ............814,311 | ................... | 740 |
| Buildings, Equipment, & Machinery .......... 1,055,657 | ................... | 960 |
| Expenses Paid in Advance ................. 73,008 | .................... | 66 |
| TOTALS ...................$3,431,927 | .............. | $3,107 |

*The per employee total of $3,107 is equivalent to over $200,000 near the end of the twentieth century.*

1937 marked another end of an era. Charles Teetor died—the last of his generation to manage the company. His eldest son Lothair, now forty, replaced him as president. Ralph assumed the title of vice president in charge of engineering.

Two years before his death, Charlie printed his code of ethics for the company. It hung in the board room for the rest of the life of the company, reflecting their continued commitment, learned from the founders, to honest management and personal responsibility.

In 1939 Ralph's father died. Although his health had been poor all his adult life, John did live to be seventy-nine years old. Kindly and gentle, he had assumed the roll of the "businessman" of the family and as such, had played his part well with the company. He had not attempted to compete with the exceptional mechanical creativity of his brother Charlie or his son Ralph. But he counseled them both in business affairs, making sure that expenses were controlled and bills collected. True, he could rarely say "no" to Charlie's sometimes harebrained investments, usually involving some land or mineral rights Charlie felt were valuable and wanted to share with the family. Flooded orange groves in Mexico, defunct gold mines in Colorado, swampland in Florida—good-natured John pitched in for most of Charlie's ideas.

Sometimes Charlie had it right. After John Teetor died, Ralph went to Florida to inspect his father's land investment there. At the time Charlie and John had bought several lots each, they had been promised that it would be developed quickly. The Depression, of course, put a crimp in those plans and the developer couldn't give Ralph assurance when houses would be built. As he stood on the land, his companions described for him the dismal swamp that surrounded them. "Sell it," he ordered. They did. A few years later that property became an integral part of booming Miami Beach.

Kate, my grandmother, lived another sixteen years until age ninety-four. I remember her as a gentle, timid, loving old lady who

## To Present and Future
# Boards of Directors

May no chair in this room ever be occupied by anyone who holds a thought, either consciously or unconsciously, of hatred, malice, revenge, dishonesty, selfishness, greed, contempt, jealousy, or any other form of thought that will be to the detriment of the Company, Board of Directors, any member of the Board, any employee or group of employees, against neighbors, townsmen or competitors.

When the Golden Rule is employed as a part of our Daily Doings our thoughts become so pure, and as a result of such thinking, so powerful that it is impossible for them to be dethroned in any way or under any condition or circumstance.

The name "Perfect Circle" was first used to designate a perfection of form to our piston ring. Later it became the name of our Company. Now, let the name "Perfect Circle" represent, surround and hold the highest ideals of man to man and with this thought ever present it will be impossible for the shadow of this Company or its Board of Directors ever to grow shorter.

January 1, 1935

Charles N. Teetor
RESIDENT

frequently worried, cautioning me to "not swing so high" or ride my bicycle so fast—which only spurred me on to greater heights and speed.

My father greeted the responsibilities of fatherhood with joy and dedication. While he traveled a great deal during my childhood, spending several evenings nearly every week in Detroit or New York, a phone call home at least once a day kept him in close touch. Mother and I never doubted that we were first in his priorities. In fact he was very protective of both of us and lovingly went to great lengths to keep us safe. Horace Marlatt was employed to travel with Ralph on all business trips and to chauffeur my father, mother, and me any place we might need to go out of town. Horace was an exceptionally good driver, having been trained to drive a Greyhound bus, and he had a marvelous sense of humor, so he, too, became surrogate family.

It was common practice in those days for a family such as ours to employ a "nanny" who also prepared the meals. When I was three, Mrs. Neva Doddridge joined our family. She was a widow with three grown daughters and several grandchildren, and I was very fond of her. The arrangement enabled Mother to travel occasionally with my father and gave her more help with the big house. I never felt that my parents relinquished their parenting responsibilities to these helpers or that I was ever not welcome with them when they were home. Mrs. Doddridge lived with us until the beginning of World War II, when, to fill her patriotic duty, she left to work at the factory.

My father and mother attended Christian Science church every Sunday and I was taken to Sunday School there. I didn't always like it (depending on who the teacher was) but staying home was not an option. Mother, a Presbyterian, never really embraced Christian Science, but I didn't know that until forty years later, so loyal was she in supporting her husband. My father did believe in Christian Science, but he was the first to call a doctor if Mother or I were ill. He even sought medical help for himself when he felt it was necessary. Even though he carried with him the knowledge that one of his eyes could have been saved if he had had immediate expert medical care like Nellie did, he had respect for Christian Science. The Christian part he was very sure about. Dad's theology was simple and straight forward. Struggling with some ethical problem at a young age, I remember asking him how he always knew what was right or wrong. He replied, "I just try to do what Jesus would have done." His philosophy obviously was deeper than that, but the answer he gave me was impressive and effective for a ten-year-old.

During these years my father taught me to roller skate, to ride a bike, to row and dock a boat. I learned the rules of football by listening with him to games on the radio. While he worked in his basement workshop I loved to play there, making "curls" by sliding a plane over a block of wood which he set up for me in a vise. He taught me to read gauges and the sizes of drills. I watched him carefully put them away in their proper places so he would know exactly where they were the next time he needed them. And sometimes he would pull out of the cupboard the miniature steam engine that he had made as a child and run it just for me with his compressed air hose. The solid chug-chugging sound of the piston and the spinning flywheel fascinated me. Later I sometimes entertained myself with the bottle of pure mercury kept in his cupboard; a few drops behaved so strangely rolling about the table, and touching the substance to a silver dime made the coin slick and shiny. Although my father cautioned me to wash my hands after I had played with the mercury, neither of us considered it to be dangerous.

While I loved playing with my dolls and "little girl" toys, I combined these activities with other interests. One special pleasure I had was running an electric train around and around a six-foot oval track, with all my dolls riding on fantastic journeys through paper mountain tunnels and enchanted clay forests. For several years at the top of my Christmas and birthday list was "more train" to enlarge the small oval track, adding track crossings and switches for a more complex layout like the one my cousin Jack had, which I so admired. Only after I was an adult did I learn from my mother that my father had firmly said, "No more train; she is a girl." It was one of the few toys that I can ever remember being denied.

About 1937 a new product came on the market which could have been invented just for my father. The electric razor increased his independence, freed him from his daily trek to the barbershop and gave him a new mechanical toy. He could finally shave himself. He was sure everyone would find this new shaver just as exciting as he did, so he gave them to all his friends. After a time new models came to the stores. He tried them all but his love affair was with Schick. Over the years he bought and distributed dozens of them to his friends.

Having heard it discussed in their own homes, my school classmates sometimes asked me if my father was blind. Until I was about ten I honestly replied, "No." I knew that he couldn't see as well as I could because he sometimes bumped into things. But he moved so confidently around the house, never mentioning that he couldn't see, that it didn't seem possible to me that he could be blind. There were rules about my not leaving my toys on the floor but my mother was by nature a very neat person, so I connected the rules to her housekeeping. In his daily living my father required less assistance than I did. Mother read to him and she read to me. She drove the car, but he frequently suggested where to turn. And my father used many expressions like "Let me see it" or "I will show you." Finally my cousin and childhood friend Connie told me about his accident, and so I learned rather like most children learn about sex or Santa. By that time I wasn't surprised, but it was still easy to forget about it.

Looking back on those days which I took for granted, I now realize that Mother handled Dad's blindness as cleverly and skillfully as he did. Although my mother had a fairly strong, outspoken personality, she let my father know he was always the head of the household. She supported his authority and his manhood. What she needed to do for him she did unobtrusively. In dressing she picked out his neckties, made sure the part in his hair was straight and that his socks matched. That was all the help he needed. His clothes were all carefully put away in the same order in his closet and drawers as they had been in his childhood, so he could pick out exactly what he wanted. At a meal she made sure his food was cut. When dining at a restaurant she frequently ordered the same thing he did and quietly cut hers, then traded plates. She might casually say, "Ralph, your water glass is quite full," or "You have a bowl of soup in front of you." When she saw he was walking a bit off course and about to bump into something, she said quietly, "Ralph, a little to your left."

She built up the man in her life in so many little ways. In a store or restaurant he always paid the bill, using a specially-made billfold that separated the various denominations of bills, so that when he pulled them out he knew exactly which denomination he was handing out. The bills he received in change he casually handed to Mother or stuffed in his pocket to be read and put away at a later time. The coins, of course, he could identify by feel.

Mother went to great lengths not to compete with my father in his areas of expertise, not that there was much danger of that in engineering! But although Mother had been very capable in science and mathematics in school, she claimed to know little about science or mechanics after she was married. In fact her standard comment when asked about her involvement in Dad's projects was, "Heavens, no. It takes all my mechanical skill to plug in the toaster."

Some of Dad's eating habits were a source of amusement for friends and family but they were the result of the same analytical process that he applied to his business affairs. At the beginning of a meal, as he picked up his napkin, he placed his hand very lightly around his place setting, noting plate, silverware, glass height and weight as well as position. From that moment he could pick up his glass or fork without groping.

Then he liked to save the best-tasting bites for last. Thus he always began eating celery from the leafy top first to the best at the bottom of the stalk. A piece of pie fell into this category too. He knew the pie would be placed on the table with the point toward him. He quietly rotated the plate to start eating at one of the back corners, again leaving the best until the last. At one formal dinner, he did this as he was talking to the important customer sitting next to him. Thinking he was being helpful, the customer reached over and straightened the pie. Ralph discovered what had occurred but not who had done it and turned the plate back the way he wanted it. His dinner-mate, thinking Ralph was mistaken, turned it back once more. Upon finding this and thinking it was a joke or the action of an overzealous waiter, Ralph asked in a booming voice, "Who keeps turning my pie?" After some embarrassment, the customer admitted his sin and both parties had a good laugh.

Dad carried a pocketwatch that chimed out the time to the minute. His chiming watches were famous, for with them he entertained every small child he met. Although the chime was not at all loud, it carried a long way. I can remember several times being backstage for some childhood performance and hearing that chime coming from the audience, as my father checked to see how soon the production would begin. He was always there, no matter how busy he was or how insignificant my part.

Friends and neighbors in the town also watched out for Ralph. Children living along his accustomed routes from his home to town or to the factory were cautioned by their parents not to leave tricycles or roller skates on the sidewalk where he might stumble.

Of course, there were times of frustration. While he was calm in public, running into a toy or a door at home could bring on a roar. His patience did have some limits.

One exception to the usual unobtrusive roll his blindness played occurred when Mother and Dad attended movies or stage shows. Mother, in a loud whisper, would give Dad a running account of the action on the screen or stage. People sitting in front of them reacted to this with irritation or amused appreciation as fit their mood, but no one within two or three seats could ignore it.

*(Top) Newspaper picture of Ralph, Clessie Cummins and his brother Don at Jacksonville, Florida, en route to Daytona, March 18, 1930.*

*(Middle) Ralph seated in the Packard at Daytona shortly before Clessie drove it for a diesel record. (Courtesy of Lyle Cummins)*

*(Bottom) Ralph and Clessie Cummins at Lake Wawasee.*

News photo of Ralph with 500 Mile Race engineers in 1926. They were described as "speed car experts who had told of new developments in race cars to the Society of Automotive Engineers at their convention at French Lick, Indiana." Left to right: (front) George T. Briggs; Frederick E. Moskovics, president Stutz Motor Car Company; Harry Miller, maker of the car which won first place 1926. (Back) William S. Harley; A. W. Herrington; Col. William G. Wall, designer of the 1912 Speedway winner; Thomas Midgley; Ralph Teetor; Fred S. Duesenberg, maker of the 1924 and 1925 winners.

Ralph Teetor, 1936.

Fred Duesenberg, famed auto builder and racer.

*A special visitor in 1934. From left to right: (Front row) John Thomas (uncle of Lowell Thomas), Charles N. Teetor, Lowell Thomas, Ralph; (Back row) George "Pop" Hanley, personnel director of Perfect Circle, Lothair Teetor, George Keagy, and William Stout.*

# SOCIETY OF AUTOMOTIVE ENGINEERS

NORTHWEST  SECTION

# ANNUAL MEETING
### and
## Reception of President and Secretary

# TUESDAY, MARCH 24
### NINETEEN THIRTY-SIX

## NEW WASHINGTON HOTEL

Dinner at 6:30          $1.50          Entertainment

## "Keeping the Automobile Industry Young."
### By Ralph R. Teetor, President

## "Automotive Engineering Conquers the World."
### By John A.C. Warner, Secretary

*This is our big meeting of the year...*
                              *Let's make it big!*
*All members are urged to attend.*
                    *Guests are cordially welcome.*
            *Make dinner reservations now.*
      *Call H.W. Drake, EL 0076, or G.E. Bock, EL 2221*

*Ralph was president of SAE in 1936.*

*The new house in Hagerstown, Indiana, a technological marvel for the time, 1936.*

*Ralph and Marjorie Teetor, 1934.*

The Christian Science Church Sunday School in about the year 1938. Marjorie was the only absentee. (Front row) Nancy Weir, David Teetor, Sarah Small, Christeen Lichtenberg, Deborah Lichtenberg. (Second row) Connie Teetor, Betty Jane Small, Jackie Snoke, Joyce Teetor. (Third row) Delia Immel, Mrs. Harold Snoke, Mrs. Charles Teetor (Leora), Millicent Snoke, Barbara Teetor. (Back row) Ben Teetor, Dick Snoke, Charles (Chuck) Teetor, Tom Teetor.

*Electric razors were new in 1936. Ralph introduced a colleague to this new toy in a hotel room in Los Angeles while attending an SAE meeting. For Ralph the electric razor was a great blessing; it enabled him to shave himself, finally!*

*One of the frst Perfect Circle advertisements in* The Saturday Evening Post, *1924.*

# Regulator

VOLUME III • PUBLISHED BY THE PERFECT CIRCLE COMPANY, LIMITED, *TORONTO, CANADA* • JULY 1936

# LOUIS MEYER WINS 500-MILE RACE
## SETS NEW TRACK RECORD OF 109.069 M.P.H.

### Every Car Finishing Race 100% Perfect Circle Equipped

● Driving a beautiful and well-timed race, Louis Meyer, the speed demon from sunny California, won the twenty-fourth 500-Mile Race at the Indianapolis Motor Speedway on Decoration Day. In winning this year's gasoline derby, Meyer hung up several new records.

Besides winning some $50,000 in prize money, he proved it was possible to win the Indianapolis classic three times, something that no driver has ever done before.

In performing this seemingly impossible feat at the astonishing speed of 109.069 M. P. H., Meyer nosed out youthful Ted Horn, driving a Hartz Special, who was 2 minutes and 17 seconds behind him. Horn's average for the five century grind was 108.170 M.P.H.

Not only did Meyer wipe out the former record but the first five cars to finish bettered Petillo's 1935 record of 106.240 M.P.H., the list including Ted Horn, Doc Mackenzie, Mauri Rose and Chet Miller who trailed the victor in the order listed.

### NEW RECORD OF 109.069 M.P.H. UPSETS THE ADVANCE DOPE

● With gasoline restricted to 37½ gallons and oil at 6 gallons for the 500 miles, most of the boys "in the know" were worried about running out of gasoline. The fact that 10 cars finished the race, some with gas to spare, proves that this race *can* be run with 37½ gallons of gasoline.

When the thirty-three cars lined up for the start of the race at 10:00 A.M. May 30th, thirty were 100% equipped with Perfect Circle Piston Rings. *Every single one of the ten cars getting the checkered flag used Perfect Circles 100%.*

With only 37½ gallons of gasoline and a minimum amount of oil allowed, these drivers knew they had to extract every ounce of power, and get the best gas and oil mileage possible from their motors, to place in the money. All were generous in praising Perfect Circle performance.

### TURN TO PAGE FOUR FOR COMPLETE DETAILS OF RACE

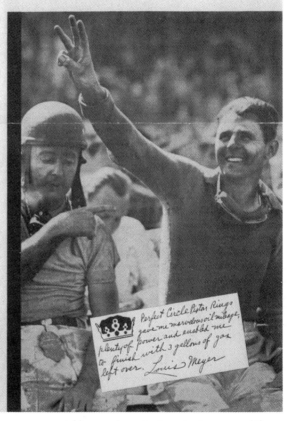

*Perfect Circle Piston Rings gave me marvelous oil mileage, plenty of power and enabled me to finish with 3 gallons of gas left over. Louis Meyer*

The Regulator *newssheet was sent to jobbers and repair shops in the automobile industry.*

# Top of the Ladder

In retrospect, one is surprised that a war with Germany was not more clearly anticipated by all who read the newspapers in Hagerstown, Indiana, as elsewhere. Many industries, including the automotive industry, were preparing war materials long before our country officially declared war after the bombing of Pearl Harbor on December 7, 1941. By the beginning of 1940, Perfect Circle's production of aircraft piston rings for defense was increasing dramatically and, as a result, Ralph Teetor's contacts with Wright Aeronautical Corporation and Allison Engineering Company had intensified. After war was declared, the U.S. found that planes, tanks, and trucks had to operate under tough conditions of desert heat and arctic cold. Engineers scrambled to solve the new problems such demands presented.

In 1942 Perfect Circle completed construction of a new building specifically for engineering and engine-testing with the latest state-of-the-art equipment. It was Ralph's pride and joy. He and the other engineers moved their offices into the new building and creative ideas flowed. Since a street separated the new building from the main factory, a pedestrian tunnel was built to connect the two areas. The tunnel walls were rough concrete, so for his guidance Ralph had a brass hand rail put on one side of the entire length of the tunnel with a gooseneck in it where the mail carts were to be stored.

Many Perfect Circle employees reported that one of the first instructions they received after they were employed was that *nothing* was ever to be left in a hallway where Ralph might stumble over it. This included boxes, mail carts, furniture—nothing. Additionally, they were not to rearrange any furniture or move any machines without informing Ralph immediately.

Production of new automobiles came to an abrupt halt in 1942, and private automobile driving was severely curtailed as the war brought rubber shortages and gasoline rationing. However, it was a year of unparalleled growth for Perfect Circle as the company converted exclusively to war production. To fulfill the requirements of the Defense Department, the company built another plant for the manufacture of aircraft rings in Richmond, Indiana. By the end of the year, ninety-seven percent of Perfect Circle's total production was used for aircraft, tanks, and trucks for the Armed Forces. The number of Perfect Circle employees more than doubled in that one year. It would double again the following year.

In November, 1942, the UAW-CIO was elected to replace the local union at Tipton, New Castle, and Hagerstown. Ralph and his cousins, ever suspicious of big, national unions, were disappointed, but they were not surprised. As the company grew larger it became a more attractive prospect for unionization. Managers at Perfect Circle had to remind each other that with so many new people being hired in such a short time, the new employees had little opportunity to understand how much Perfect Circle management cared and valued fairness. The old collegial atmosphere had fallen victim to fast industrial growth and to wartime pressures for increased production.

According to the 1943 annual report, Perfect Circle attained in that year its all-time peak in both production and numbers of employees. Total employment reached 6,455, of which 52.5 percent were women, many taking the place of their fighting husbands and brothers. Production capacity was used exclusively for war work and essential domestic replacement. Perfect Circle rings were used in submarines, patrol boats, tanks, army trucks, and thousands of miscellaneous engines used in the war. Millions more of the rings were supplied for tractors, trucks, buses, and cars for essential domestic transportation. To prevent sabotage, everyone entering the factories wore an official badge and visitors were closely scrutinized. It seemed odd in a town where everyone had always known each other and still did.

The auto companies, too, were producing exclusively for military use. Ralph had been accustomed to trading at least one of his two cars each year for the newest and latest technology developed by his friends at General Motors. Thrifty Nellie claimed that the best effect of the war shortages was that she and Ralph finally got their money's worth out of their cars—for several years Ralph couldn't trade his still soundly-running cars for new ones.

Ralph's work with the SAE War Engineering Board, where studies determined that chrome plating piston rings prolonged their efficiency in engines under desert conditions, has already been described. As the piston ring expert of SAE, in early 1945 he was called upon to help with another matter. This time New Zealand was trying to give protected status to its local companies by prohibiting import of similar products from other countries. General Motors was exporting cars and replacement piston rings to New Zealand, when New Zealand told GM that their piston rings would no longer be accepted, because a local company was now manufacturing them. "We protested and put up an argument that we cannot blithely accept unknown rings in place of a product which has been thoroughly tested and approved by various factories for use in the respective engines," wrote W. D. Appel, chief engineer of General Motors Overseas Division, to Ralph in January of 1945. "But the New Zealand government seems to feel that tests conducted by their National Physical Laboratory should be valid as the deciding factor in the issue." However, no provision was made for dynamometer or road testing. Not only did GM believe the testing and specifications inadequate, but the company also feared that the policy would spread to other products and even other countries. They asked Ralph for help. Realizing the importance of the matter to Perfect Circle, he readily gave his support.

Since most standards for automotive components were written by SAE, Ralph drew the prestige of the whole War Engineering Board behind his reply. He pointed out that because each engine model is different, there is no simple test to compare the functional qualifications of piston rings for a group of engines.

*The best types and combinations of rings must be selected for each engine model through extensive testing. Some of the physical and metallurgical specifications of piston rings are so critical that engine manufacturers will not interchange rings made under the same specifications by different ring manufacturers without running extensive engine tests. Thus the Society of Automotive Engineers cannot offer a uniform procedure of testing piston rings for all engines.*

It appears that ended the problem.

The war overshadowed Teetor family life: victory gardens, rationing of meat, sugar, shoes, and gasoline, along with shortages of almost everything, dominated daily experience. Ralph worked long hours developing ways to make the engines of the United States military machine more durable and efficient. Hagerstown and all America suspended travel and saved fuel to support the soldiers and win the war. Nellie knitted socks and sweaters, folded bandages, learned first aid and mailed off boxes of cookies to strange places. The first aid courses she taught required her to wear the only pair of slacks she ever owned. Everyone was in "the war effort." Only Shib was left to help Nellie with a house that was too much for her to care for alone.

But poor Shib was almost spirited away the morning following the Pearl Harbor attack. Two FBI agents appeared at the door, asking Nellie about Shib, now an "enemy alien." Would she continue to employ him? Of course. Where did he live? Where did he eat? Where did he go on his days off? The federal agents scribbled the answers on their writing pads. After asking her to notify them if anything changed, the FBI agents left, never to return. Shib was as loyal to the United States as the most patriotic native-born. He would have become a naturalized citizen years before, if our laws had not prohibited the Japanese from doing so. But after Pearl Harbor there was a growing undercurrent of resentment toward Shib among some folks in the town who didn't know him. Ralph and Nellie became concerned for his safety, so they arranged for him to move into a room in the big house. It was his home for the next twenty years until he retired.

In the spirit of all-out support, *The Circle* employee newsletter was renamed *The Victory Circle*. Management continued to print its views on current affairs and the employment outlook for the company for the upcoming weeks as well as to keep employees informed on regulations coming from Washington. Although they tried to present all the new government regulations in very positive language, the New Deal legislation in general continued to rankle, provoking this item:

*Horse Sense: The war on private enterprise (the American way of business) that is shaping up in Washington—and which is purely socialistic in origin and has nothing to do with our war effort—has been brilliantly condemned in a dairy trade publication,* Land o' Lakes News:

1. *You cannot bring about prosperity by discouraging thrift.*
2. *You cannot strengthen the weak by weakening the strong.*
3. *You cannot help small men by tearing down big men.*
4. *You cannot help the poor by destroying the rich.*
5. *You cannot lift the wage-earner by pulling the wage-payer down.*
6. *You cannot keep out of trouble by spending more than your income.*
7. *You cannot further the brotherhood of man by inciting class hatred.*
8. *You cannot establish sound security on borrowed money.*
9. *You cannot build character and courage by taking away man's initiative and independence.*
10. *You cannot help men permanently by doing for them what they could and should do for themselves.*

Programs mandated by the federal government grew, and with them Ralph's conviction that government should not intrude in people's lives and businesses. He was always alert to find ways to enhance the education of young people in the fundamental principles of business, economics, and traditional work ethics. No wonder he was excited when he attended a National Association of Manufacturers (NAM) meeting in New York in 1939 which featured a little known business education enterprise called Junior Achievement.

Junior Achievement was originated about 1919 by Horace Moses, president of Swathmore Paper Company in Springfield, Massachusetts. It was intended to give the urban youth opportunities similar to those that 4-H clubs offered rural young people. Members began by creating handicraft articles, but over time the organization became increasingly business-oriented and produced more practical products, while providing free enterprise business management experience for its participants. In 1939 Charles Hook, president of Armco Steel and of the National Association of Manufacturers, called together about fifty company leaders to promote Junior Achievement nationwide. I remember how enthusiastically my father described to me the student-run businesses when he returned home from that dinner. World War II delayed national promotion of Junior Achievement, but the group met again in New York after the war to incorporate the National Junior Achievement program in 1947. Ralph served on the national Board of Directors, promoting and encouraging the program throughout Indiana. It was a proud moment when his home town, Hagerstown, finally opened a Junior Achievement Center in 1970.

At the end of World War II the soldiers came home, some resuming their lives just where they had left them, others living with the reality that their lives could never be the same. Ralph's final wartime contribution was a speech delivered to veterans who had lost their sight fighting for their country's freedom. Excerpts were recorded in a press release sent out by the public relations office of the Army:

*Phoenixville, Pa.—July 12, 1945—Ralph Teetor, prominent automotive engineer and former president of the Society of Automotive Engineers, who has been sightless since the age of five, addressed 200 blind veterans of this war at the Valley Forge General Hospital this week, telling them that "nothing can stop you from enjoying a normal, happy life once you have made up your mind that is what you are going to have."*

*Now a member of the War Engineering Board, Mr. Teetor lost his sight following an accident in 1895. He was graduated from the Engineering School of the University of Pennsylvania in 1912 and embarked immediately upon his career in automotive engineering. During World War I, he developed a procedure for balancing turbine rotors in destroyers that still is used today.*

*"In all of your experiences from now on," Mr. Teetor told his audience, "you will find that you have to 'sell' yourself to almost every person*

*that you meet. People will doubt your ability to do a job, but you must convince them that not only can you do that job, but also you can do it as well as anyone else.*

*"Choose the field for which you feel you are qualified. Work hard to learn as much as you can about it. When you feel you are ready, go for it.*

*"Remember, you are not handicapped so long as you can think logically. You will be handicapped only if you are slovenly in your thinking.*

*"Many times during the past forty-nine years people have told me how sorry they were that I am 'handicapped.' My answer to them always has been that I am not handicapped, because I have never considered myself so.*

*"If anyone in the whole world has had more fun out of life than I have had, I should like to meet him. I am sure no one has enjoyed living more than I.*

*"It will take courage and hard work for you to become accustomed to your new way of life. But you will make it by holding your heads high and never allowing yourselves to falter."*

Ralph had lived these words of advice.

My father did counsel a few individuals who had lost the use of their eyes, especially at the end of this war, though he never discussed even with his family what advice he gave. One of these individuals was Tom Hasbrook, a war veteran who, at age twenty-four, was returning to a young wife expecting their first baby. The young veteran was wondering what the next fifty or so years could possibly hold for him when his father-in-law took him to visit Ralph. "I remember we spent a couple of hours at his house in Hagerstown," Tom related. "He showed me what he had been able to accomplish. I was really impressed by what he had done, and he encouraged me to decide what I wanted to do and work for it." Tom must have taken that advice to heart, because he achieved an outstanding career in industry and in government, encouraging and inspiring others in turn.

Ralph frequently inspired the sighted too. Myron Hunt, a long-time engineer for Perfect Circle, recounts his first meeting with Ralph. "I had worked for Perfect Circle just a short time when I attended a meeting in Detroit. That evening I was in the lobby of the hotel wondering where I would eat supper, when Ralph and Horace Marlatt walked in. I knew Horace but not Ralph. After I said 'hello' to them, Horace asked me if I would have dinner with Ralph because he had an errand he needed to do. I gulped! I was new in the organization and a young guy, and here was a man of great stature! I told Horace I would be happy to but I didn't know what I would do.

"After a little conversation Ralph suggested that we go over to the Detroit Athletic Club for supper. I replied that I would be glad to, but I didn't know where it was. 'I'll show you,' he said. He took my arm and we dogtrotted the four blocks to the Detroit Athletic Club. We turned the corner, hiked up the stairs and walked straight to the maître d'. It was amazing to me."


The end of the war meant a summer of celebration at Lake Wawasee. To save precious gasoline and rubber tires and to show support for our soldiers, most of the "summer people" had stayed home during the war. It just didn't seem right to be playing when so many people were sacrificing so much. With the war over, the summer of 1946 was a grand reunion of Teetor cousins and friends, a continuous house party to which everyone came. The Teetor cottages at Wawasee bulged with guests coming and going. The old wooden speedboats, always Chris Crafts, came out of storage and were polished until they fairly glowed. Sails were hoisted on the sailboats, and everyone under the age of thirty-five was trying to master the new challenge of water skiing. For most of us this first postwar summer was pure play.

One day Dan stood on his pier taking movies of Jack and his friends water skiing. George Sommer, later president of CTS Corporation, was driving the boat for this "Hollywood" review. Dan directed George to pull the skiers past the pier about twenty-five feet from the end while he photographed. George said he would try but he wasn't sure how to judge twenty-five feet. Ralph happened to be standing nearby and, hearing them, he said, "Oh, that isn't too difficult. This pier is exactly fifty feet long so if you will just visualize this pier half again longer, you will know the spot to drive the boat." When Jack told this story he ended with the comment, "Uncle Ralph was always solving sighted problems for people who could see."

One of Ralph's most frequently mentioned philosophies was the interconnectedness of people's lives. The example he frequently used was the making of a common wooden lead pencil. He would begin, "Just think of the many different people whom we depend on to provide us with that lead pencil: people who mined, refined, and shaped the graphite, the people who logged the wood, milled it, painted it, made the paint, built the tools. The list of people required to make a common lead pencil is practically infinite. Then all those people depend on our buying the pencil which starts our money back through the chain." Perhaps it was a way that he dealt with his obvious need for occasional help from others without giving up his sense of adequacy.

It is not always possible to determine when Ralph began to invent a new product. Ideas brewed in his mind for years and then suddenly burst forth as projects. The idea for a new door lock came from an illustration that Ralph used in his counseling. He would insist to blind people that self-pity was their greatest enemy. Rather than considering themselves handicapped they should honestly concede that they are merely inconvenienced at times. He used this illustration. "Suppose you arrive at your front door with your arms full of packages after you have been shopping. It is an inconvenience that you do not have a third hand to open the door, but you wouldn't consider yourself handicapped or feel sorry for yourself because you lack three hands. You must learn to consider your blindness in the same way, an inconvenience at times but no cause for self-pity." That set his fertile mind thinking. Why do we have to turn the door knob to open the door? If our hands were full at the moment it would be much easier if we could open the door by just pushing on the knob—or pulling to go the other way. At several times over the years Ralph "tinkered" with this problem in his basement workshop. What emerged was a mechanism simpler than the conventional door lock, with a third as many moving parts. A slight pressure on the knob allowed the catch to move in and out of the keeper with a rocking action that was not possible to jam. The lock, however, had two drawbacks: it did not work well if the door did not fit properly in its frame. Ralph always made sure his doors fit very well so he didn't take that problem very seriously. The other objection was that the device was somewhat difficult to lock, but that difficulty, he was sure, could be overcome.

Ralph's development work on the door lock intensified after World War II. He expected to take advantage of the building boom that followed the war but it actually worked against him. At that time so much was being built so fast that the lock companies were able to sell everything they could make. They could not see any advantage to introducing a brand-new product requiring retooling and extensive advertising at a time when they were already busy with orders. Ralph collected four patents for the door lock between 1950 and 1953. He installed a few of the latches on his home and office doors so he could demonstrate it. After making some sincere attempts to sell the lock, he left it, hoping some new enthusiasm would appear for it later. He was also developing the Speedostat at the same time, which for him was a much higher priority.

The end of the war created many strains in the industrial world, with the country switching back to peacetime pursuits. Producers of essential war products like the automotive industry had to shrink their production capacities, as well as convert to peacetime products. After several years of patching, repairing, and making do without new consumer products, people had tremendous pent-up desires to buy new things. The market exploded as people replaced whatever was old and worn out with new and shiny merchandise. Innovations developed during the war such as nylon and synthetic fabrics, automatic washing machines and dryers, and frozen food, soon found their way to store shelves and showroom floors. Families reunited with their servicemen fathers, sons, and brothers. Husbands and wives were together again, and the automobile, symbol of individualism and freedom, now played to family image, mobility, and recreation. The station wagon was king.

Perfect Circle shed its wartime schedule and returned to its former size. But with piston rings now far more durable and long-lasting, it was critical that this company, too, expand its markets with new products, most of which the engineers invented in their own laboratory and tool room.

Sometimes a new proposal came from outside the company. One such product brought to Perfect Circle by its inventor was a mysterious liquid which, when added to the oil in an automobile engine, was supposed to enhance engine performance and increase gasoline mileage significantly. Its claims were impressive, and executives at Perfect Circle enthusiastically planned for a new and very different product. While completing plans to test its engine-enhancing claims, Perfect Circle initiated procedures to organize a new company division called the Teetor Company to market the additive. The tests would be conducted at the Indianapolis Motor Speedway by driving thirty cars, both old and new models, three hundred miles at fifty miles per hour. Don Teetor's son Tom drove one of the cars, in what was a practical, scientific test. They drove half the distance, one hundred fifty miles, without the additive. Then they added the new substance and drove another one hundred fifty miles. The test results showed absolutely no difference in performance. Ralph snorted that there were snake oil salesmen in the automotive business too and scrapped the plans for the new division.

Testing was only one of the relationships Perfect Circle had with the Speedway. The famous 500 Mile Race had been a major promotional event for the company almost from the time the track was built. Because so many early automobile companies originated in Indiana, Carl Fisher and three fellow investors built the two-and-a-half-mile track in Indianapolis for those companies to test, race, and promote their cars. The first attempts were far from successful. Ralph was there to witness the bizarre happenings which characterized early races. He remembered that on the first dirt track, clouds of dust created by the racing cars cut visibility to nearly zero, causing several serious accidents before the race was stopped. Two years later the track was paved with brick and the race lengthened to five hundred miles. The Perfect Circle band played for that first 500 Mile Race in 1911 and every subsequent one until World War II. Since these races tested and advertised not only the automobiles themselves but also parts such as piston rings, each year it mattered whether the winner had Perfect Circle piston rings in his car. Equally important were the statistics of how many cars with Perfect Circle parts finished the five hundred miles or dropped out with mechanical breakdown. Perfect Circle engineers worked long and hard with the engine builders and drivers such as Harry Miller, Fred Duesenberg, and Wilbur Shaw to help them produce the finest, most powerful racing machines. Woody Ulrich, who worked closely with Ralph for years, relates, "the race drivers would bring their engine blocks in to Ralph to have the rings installed. If he approved the job, they knew it was as near perfect as it could possibly be."

The first Perfect Circle-equipped winner, Jimmy Murphy, scored in 1922 and Tommie Milton equalled the performance in 1923. After that Perfect Circle-equipped cars usually won the race and dominated the number of finishers, giving the company something to advertise all over the country. But there were a number of other companies who made piston rings, so the threat of stiff competition always lurked nearby.

In 1937, the year that Wilbur Shaw won his first of three victories, Ralph served as chief steward of the 500. William S. Knudson, president of General Motors, Charles Merz of Indianapolis, and Ralph composed the board which ruled on any protests or other race questions which might arise. Later, when racing halted during World War II, the great racing oval was in grave danger of closing forever. When the war ended, Wilbur Shaw convinced Tony Hulman, Jr., to purchase the track from Eddie Rickenbacker. For the next several years Perfect Circle was a major sponsor of the race as well as the famous radio broadcast featuring Sid Collins, bringing the thrilling progress of the race into living rooms around the country.

Many commonplace automotive safety devices, such as rearview mirrors, shatterproof glass, and seat belts were first developed and tested at the Speedway. The oval showcased continuous improvements in engines, brakes, tires, and shock absorbers, really every element of automotive design. Ralph loved the mechanical innovations and challenges the race offered.

He was less enthusiastic about attending the race itself. Still, he couldn't stay away as long as he was physically able to be there. Even in his later years he was glued to the radio for the entire performance.


Ralph's restless creativity touched almost everything he did during the forties. The extensive landscaping on the ten acres surrounding his beautiful home involved monumental amounts of grass cutting and maintenance. After researching the available lawn mowers and trying all that seemed most suitable, he couldn't find one that really pleased him. That simply meant that he would have to invent a better one. On July 3, 1945 he wrote his friend and patent attorney:

*Dear Harry,*

*You will recall that during the last several visits we have had, I have discussed with you a new type of lawn mower. For some time I have been doing considerable work on this device and now have an experimental cutter unit under construction which employs the new idea. I believe the cutting element is new and I would like to prepare and file a patent application to cover the principles employed.*

*I am enclosing a sketch which I believe will clearly show the general construction of the new cutter. It consists of an endless metal belt which is carried over two pulleys, one at each side of the vehicle of a more or less conventional lawn mower. The pulleys on which the steel belt runs have their axles in approximately horizontal position, and one of the pulleys is rotated by either a separate power source, or if no mechanical power is employed, by being geared to one or both of the vehicle's wheels. The steel belt has cut in the front edge a series of teeth similar to a band saw and the straight portion of it which runs between the bottom side of each pulley also runs between the stationary toothed guards. This mechanism is located so that when the mower is driven or pushed forward, the teeth in the guards will be pushed into the grass and at the same time the teeth in the flexible saw, which is being run between the guards, will clip the grass.*

*I own mowers which use the only two general types of cutters available at this time, and find the following limitations of each: the reel or rotary type of cutter is limited in the height of grass it will cut. When the grass has grown to a height in excess of half of the diameter of the cutter, it will not satisfactorily cut the grass, for it will fail to feed into the cutter and will only be knocked down by it.*

*The other principle type of cutting unit generally used is the oscillating sickle such as is used in large power and horse-drawn mowers used for cutting crops of hay, etc. This type of cutter has the advantage of being able to cut tall grass, but it has the disadvantage of leaving the mowed surface very rough and jagged. In this type of cutter one of the toothed elements oscillates over the other toothed element which causes the teeth to pass each other and shear the grass. The trouble with this cutter is that the cutting element must stop and reverse its motions at each end of the travel while the cutter advances. . . .*

*With the scheme I propose, the saw or cutter will operate continuously and can be driven without difficulty at much higher speeds than the oscillating type of cutter, so that it will cut practically continuously along the constant advance of the mower.*

Perfect Circle, like most companies, demanded first claim on all patents and improvements developed by its employees, releasing those to the inventors which it had no interest in developing. Ralph soon got his release of patent ownership, but he found that persuading someone to manufacture an entirely new mower was more difficult than inventing it. Besides, he had other things that were more interesting to pursue. Many of his friends breathed a sigh of relief when he put away the lawn mower project. They had found it unnerving to watch him demonstrate how his mower worked, running his fingers so close to the lethally-sharp cutting edges.

Nineteen forty-six marked a major change in Ralph Teetor's life; he became president of Perfect Circle, replacing Lothair Teetor. While he enjoyed the opportunities for a broader influence in the company's progress, being president was not what he had sought or was destined to enjoy. Engineering was his first and only real love in the workplace; now he had to come out of "the laboratory" and sit behind a desk. While he continued to spend as much time in engineering as he could, obligations of the presidency demanded much of his energy now. He did, however, take advantage of the additional opportunities which the presidency gave him to develop and promote some of his favorite philosophies. He started on his first day in his new office with the following letter to all the employees.

*A MESSAGE TO EVERY MEMBER OF THE PERFECT CIRCLE ORGANIZA-TION—FROM YOUR NEW PRESIDENT*

*Naturally you want to know what your president thinks about his job—what his chief interests are, what his convictions are and what principles of management he intends to follow.*

*This letter, therefore, is not only a message to the members of Perfect Circle Company. It is also an invitation to every one of you to express yourself to me and to other members of management.*

*Of course, I come to my job with some convictions and a respect for certain principles which I shall attempt to express here.*

*First, I think we can all agree that a very sound, substantial business has been created. Perfect Circle has shown consistent growth since its founding fifty-one years ago. It has withstood the strains of three wars, a major Depression, and many smaller business recessions. Our previous leaders deserve much credit for this achievement.*

*The second point with which there can be no disagreement is that we have not arrived at a state of perfection! And we probably never will.*

*My third belief is that the existing world forces will either compel us to rise to new heights of organizational strength or will seriously weaken our present structure.*

*My fourth conviction is that the Perfect Circle group possesses the intelligence, the capacity, the will, and the ingenuity to cope successfully with our problems. I have no doubt that it will develop the strength needed for the days ahead.*

*What is the truly social objective of any industrial organization? Don't you agree that it is the fair and just balance between the interests of customers, workers, managers, and investors? We can be sure of this—an equitable balance will be approached only if each of these interests is willing to give broad and genuine consideration to the others.*

*My training and experience as an engineer have required that I obey the principles of physical science. It is my belief that there are corresponding principles of human relations which, if generally accepted and practiced, would guide us to solutions of our social problems. These are merely the simple rules of conduct: sincere consideration, honesty, patience, generosity, and mutual confidence. All groups must practice these principles willingly to establish better understanding. They cannot be forced by laws.*

*Volumes have been written about the techniques of management. Many of them contain excellent organizational plans. But I am convinced that without a willingness on the part of each member of the group to put himself in the other fellow's shoes, no organization will have the strength to survive and to progress in our highly competitive society.*

*The struggle to live by these principles of human relations is the most difficult problem that any one of us faces. I expect to be reminded of my own faults in following these principles and do my utmost to continue to promote their general acceptance throughout the entire organization.*

> *Ralph R. Teetor*
> *March 21, 1946*

Ralph still had faith in people's good judgment. All they needed was sound information to make informed decisions. To this end he spoke and wrote freely, giving his opinions. In 1947 William McGarry wrote a short biographical sketch of Ralph for the book he was putting together, *Tomorrow's Leaders*, in which he quoted some of Ralph's ideas:

*The founding ancestors of this business [Perfect Circle] were pioneers. They got what they had by working for it, beginning at the beginning—in the soil. They cut down the trees and quarried the rock for their homes and barns. They cleared the land for their farms. They made their own tools at hand forges.*

*I am not advocating the repetition of that for all our young men and women of today. It isn't necessary even if it were possible. But I do believe our schools and colleges are turning out students who take the nation's vast industrial plant for granted. Many of them act as if they thought it just grew and had always been there.*

*How can youngsters know what went into building this country— since they do not have to pioneer in the same fields—if they are not taught?*

*How can they benefit from the national industrial economy if they do not understand what is essential to keep it running, particularly when they must contribute to it?*

*Engineering was made easy for me by one of the most inspiring men I've ever met, the late Professor Henry Spangler. He hammered on the fundamental laws of thermodynamics. I think we have to follow that procedure in human relations if we are to rid ourselves of the misunderstandings that lead to so many unnecessary disputes.*

*What we have done in this country industrially is a wonder of the modern world. But what we haven't done is still a bigger job. Nothing is perfect. Everything can be improved. The certain way to continued progress is education, beginning at the beginning with our youth, but making it emphatic that the process never ends.*

This was Ralph's sincere philosophy of personal relationships, which he believed should also determine management decisions. Having watched the negotiations in Detroit, he was apprehensive about the labor movement's adversarial influence on employee-management relationships. But the union had come to Perfect Circle, and it remained to be seen how it would affect workers' lives and the future of the company. The first peacetime contract negotiations between Perfect Circle and the CIO started in late September, 1947, and lasted five months before a contract was signed. Only a few months later the union was back to the bargaining table, demanding more. This resulted in a strike lasting most of November and December of 1948. The issues were a few cents an hour increase in wages and the union shop—the requirement that all employees paid dues to the union whether they wished to join or not. To Ralph and the rest of management, accepting union shop would have meant betrayal of the rights and freedom of their employees, requiring them to support a cause that some did not approve of. The union gave up this time, but they would try again in a few years.

As the seven weeks of the strike passed, Ralph would calculate the number of hours, then weeks and months, that the strikers had to work to gain back the wages which they lost while they were on strike, even if they got all they were asking for. "The potential payback is so meager," he said, sadly. "At most the difference between proposals of management and union is eight cents an hour. If employees get the whole eight cents they gain only $3.20 a week. In the seven week strike our lowest paid workers lost $378 in wages. It will take them two and a half *years* just to make that back at the higher wage." Nearly half the employees seemed to understand this and willingly crossed the picket lines to come to work. The company did not suffer financially from the strike; in fact that year they set a new record for sales and profits. But over the next few years Ralph watched with increasing concern as the big automobile companies gave in to one major union demand after another, especially as they agreed to a union shop. This severely disappointed him, for he knew that eventually the increased union pressure would filter down to Perfect Circle again.

Early in 1949 Ralph began writing an editorial column in *The Circle* newsletter. In a chatty format he discussed various topics he considered of interest. In his first column in January, he informed readers of the unique importance of the Society of Automotive Engineers of which he had been national president in 1936, fourteen years before.

*I sincerely believe that the Society has been more responsible for the building of our present high class automobiles and the unusual degree of convenience for automobile drivers than any other group in the industry.*

*Did you ever stop to think about the tremendous cooperative effort necessary for you to be able to drive your car across the country? Anywhere you go, whether it be New Mexico or New York, you can buy gasoline or oil that is just right for it. You can buy tires that will fit your automobile, regardless of the make or model.*

*This didn't just happen. It is only possible because the automobile and engine manufacturers, the petroleum and tire manufacturers, and many other similar groups cooperated, mainly through SAE, to establish standardized products.*

*Standardization of screw threads, nuts, bolts, mountings, light bulbs, and many other things has not only created convenience but has saved automobile manufacturers and owners millions of dollars.*

Ralph enjoyed keeping up with technology, even though that could be demanding in the new atomic age that had now arrived. In March Ralph wrote a rather remarkable account of a fascinating experience:

> *Last week I attended a very unusual ceremony in New York City which I thought you might be interested in hearing about. It was the laying of the cornerstone for the new nineteen-story Crowell-Collier Publishing Company building. This building adjoins the big Radio City Building.*
>
> *That cornerstone was put into place by atomic energy rather than by human hands. It was the first time in history that this has ever been done.*
>
> *The two-ton cornerstone was lowered into position at the end of a chain attached to a motor atop a hoist, which was powered by energy produced by splitting ten U-235 atoms. A miniature reactor, an amplifier, and two relays were used. One relay was attached to the hoist motor and the other to a magnesium flare imbedded in a ceremonial ribbon stretched between the motor and the suspended cornerstone. A half gram of radium-beryllium was used as the neutronic source for bombarding the uranium-235. Each time a neutron struck one of the atoms, the latter was split, releasing 200,000,000 volts of energy. We heard a pronounced click as this energy, picked up by the amplifier, caused a gong to ring and a 100-watt fluorescent lamp to flash.*
>
> *This happened each time one of the ten atoms was split. After this the accumulated electrical impulse was transmitted to the motor and the magnesium flare. The ribbon broke with a loud report and bright flash. The activated motor lowered the cornerstone into position.*
>
> *This part of the occasion was quite spectacular in itself, but more so in its significance. It symbolized the beginning of an amazing era—the era of adapting atomic energy to constructive peacetime service.*

It is sometimes hard to remember that all these columns were written by a man who could not see. Ralph wrote this one for the May issue:

*Recently I heard General Joseph T. McNarney, Commander of the U.S. Air Forces, tell of some of the latest Air Force Research and Development activities.*

*His remarks about guided missiles immediately reminded me of the part this company had in the early development of this weapon. Many people think that guided missiles are only of recent concern. Actually, though, work on these missiles was started thirty-one years ago [in 1918] by "Boss" Kettering of General Motors in conjunction with the Air Corps . . .*

*The "aerial torpedoes," as they were called then, were launched from little cars which ran on a track runway. The light wheels used on these cars were the pedal car wheels which our company was making at that time.*

Since then the Air Force has come a long way in the development of guided missiles.

Several of Ralph's columns this year warned of the evils of encroaching socialism, which he believed President Truman was promoting through higher taxes and more government control of business and private lives. He also strongly opposed federal aid to education and frequently wrote, not only to Indiana legislators but also to every Congressman, promulgating his views on some current bill that he felt important. One of his letters to Congress was the topic of a column to the employees:

*Have you ever expressed your views on certain legislation to your Congressmen? Many people think it is a waste of time to write letters to our Senators and Representatives in both State and Federal governments. I can't agree with them.*

*All letters don't have to represent a partisan opinion. Our government's trend toward Socialism, for example, is not a party problem. Both Democrats and Republicans need to be vitally concerned.*

*For instance one of the bills now being considered is Federal Aid to Education. I am concerned about the effect it will have on our educational system, and I have written my viewpoint to every Senator and Representative in Congress.*

*It is true that there is not enough money spent for education purposes in any state. All need more. But Federal government participation as pro-*

*posed is not going to make more money available more easily. The money must come from exactly the same source it does now—from all the people. [Bill] S246 simply takes from Indiana money that could be used to improve our schools and passes it along to other states' schools with lower standards. This would only serve to equalize education standards throughout the country rather than improve the general standards.*

This same year, 1949, Ralph was invited to serve on the board of trustees of Earlham College, the small, academically excellent Quaker school in Richmond, Indiana. He was the first trustee in the one-hundred-two-year history of the college who was neither Quaker nor an alumnus. The college's president Tom Jones soon had an enthusiastic ally in creating a new base of financial support for private colleges. The impetus for independence from the increasing federal aid to colleges and universities, aid which had restrictive strings, came from some of the presidents themselves. Dr. Jones and Dr. Frank Sparks, President of Wabash College, were looking for ways to join the interests and concerns of business and private colleges in Indiana. With the help of Ralph and a few others, Associated Colleges of Indiana was formed. It paired each college president with one businessman to solicit businesses for contributions benefiting all the private colleges in Indiana. As the businessmen learned about academe, college presidents were listening to the educational concerns of the businessmen. This endeavor was so successful that it spread to every state in the nation.

With these new obligations, the conditions on college campuses around the country attracted more of my father's attention. It became the subject of his August, 1949, *Circle* column. For this Ralph chose to quote another spokesman, a typical strategy when he found someone who expressed his exact views more eloquently than he felt he himself could:

*Very frequently we hear sharp criticism of the ideas our schools, colleges, and universities are teaching. People point to many un-American doctrines which are being taught to the students in some of these institutions. Unfortunately, some of this criticism is justified; however, I find that* many of our schools are teaching sound principles.

A few weeks ago I had the opportunity to read the commencement address to the graduating class of Northwestern University, presented by the President of the University, Dr. Franklin B. Snyder. It was certainly gratifying to me to know some of the thinking of the head of that University.

"I hope that fifty years from now freedom will still exist in this land of ours. I hope that we shall not have been enslaved by either an all-powerful federal government in Washington, or by debt, much of it incurred in the name of a vague concept called 'security,' which will inevitably crush all initiative. I have no objection to paying a debt incurred in the defense of our country against Germany and Japan, nor to providing proper security for the aged and the infirm. But I do not wish to be taxed so that my grandchildren need not work for a living or pay their doctors' bills.

"The concept of freedom which we Americans cherish is a many-sided one. It implies freedom to fail as well as to succeed. We learned long ago that the rewards of victory are tawdry indeed unless they are won under the hazard of defeat. Who would watch a football game with only one team on the field? Yet that is precisely the condition that some of our social planners would like to see established. They would remove all elements of conflict, of struggle, of hazard from life; or, as they put it, they would extend security 'from the cradle to the grave.'

"Too many of us are asking the federal government to do for us what our grandparents would have done for themselves; too many office holders are keeping themselves in power by promising spectacular gifts to the electorate. The old concepts of thrift and economy are laughed out of court by theorists who delight in squandering money that other people have earned. What seems to be a wasteful and inefficient federal government is reaching out like an octopus to wrap itself around more and more phases of your life and mine."

The prophecies of these education-minded leaders of 1949 have an eerie ring of truth today.

Ralph put his own spin on the problems in education about a year later in a speech he gave for an Earlham symposium examining "A Free Society in a Free World":

*Industry has done a great job in its technological development. We have been able to manufacture more and better things than ever before. The automobile can be purchased by almost every wage earner actually at a price that is less per pound that we pay for butter. In radio it is possible for one person to speak to everyone in the world. We can carry people with the speed of sound. But with all these great developments of which there are thousands more examples, we haven't been able to make people happy or satisfied.*

*My background being engineering and research, my first question is, why? What have we missed that has divided people, creating hatred and turmoil in the world? You hear it every day on the radio, read it in the newspaper. Perhaps we have failed to teach the people to use or appreciate the things we have made. Perhaps we need to train greater leaders . . .*

Ralph then pointed out that the small, liberal arts colleges were in the best position to search for some of these answers, and to instill in their students a desire to solve the perplexing problems of society. They were the ideal laboratories to replace some of the current economic, political, and social expediencies with more wisdom and understanding and to lead society to a more harmonious world. Ralph also concerned himself, gladly I think, with the educational needs of a teenage daughter.

I grew through my teens in the 1940s, adventuresome and romantic, sometimes rebellious. My parents were loving and indulgent, but still very cautious when safety was involved. Most of my Teetor cousins were sent to boarding school by ninth grade. I was, thankfully, allowed to stay home and graduate from the Hagerstown public schools.

A major event, of course, was gaining my driver's license when I was sixteen. Horace Marlatt was assigned to teach me to drive. My parents didn't approve of a sixteen-year-old having her own car, so I was assigned our seven-passenger Cadillac. It had two jump seats which could be pulled out behind the front seat. It looked like a hearse and I hated it. My father thought if I could get it around the corners and into the parking places, I could handle anything that would come along. I think, because of its size and weight, he also considered it the safest car. I swore then that when I could finally get my own car it would be nothing fancier than a Chevrolet, and I kept that vow for decades.

The problem, as I saw it, was that this big car did nothing for my social life. I lived in the biggest house in town, and it was already hard for me to convince my friends that I was just one of the gang. The car only made my situation worse. For the most part, my complaints fell on deaf ears. My father had never been "one of the gang" and he did not care to try. Like most teenagers, I survived with few scars, having learned more humility and empathy for others than I might otherwise have gained.

Commercial air travel became commonplace after the war. Dad claimed he understood it too well to be completely comfortable with flying. He knew how many things could go wrong. While he and Mother flew many places in later years, they never flew on the same plane at the same time until after I was married, except on the few occasions when I was along. Friends who flew with Dad related that occasionally he would become very quiet, listening to the engines. If there was some problem, he always knew what it was.

After Dad became president of the company, he traveled to Detroit less and worked in his basement workshop more. Typically he came home from work at five o'clock, frequently bringing one of the engineers from the factory with him. They discussed business for an hour or so before dinner. Otherwise, Dad listened to Lowell Thomas and other newscasters on the radio. After dinner, when the events of the day had been fully shared among the family and dealt with, he spent the rest of the evening, sometimes until late at night, tinkering in his workshop. Many were the nights my mother went to bed and, wakening several hours later, walked to the top of the basement stairs to listen for Ralph who was still working on one of his "ideas" in his shop, checking to be sure that he was all right. He frequently worked in the dark; rarely did he bother to turn on a light unless someone else came down. This spooked many of his friends, who were surprised by

Dad's turning on the lights for them when they arrived, so he could show them what he was doing.

There were no special safety shields on his machines and fellow engineers marveled at the skill with which Ralph ran them. The workshop contained many drawers and cabinets for accessories and supplies, so that he knew exactly where everything was. Although he used jo-blocks with micrometers, calibers, and rulers, his best measuring instrument was his sense of touch. He astounded other mechanics when, examining some part with his fingers, he remarked, "That's pretty good, only a couple of thousandths too large." That sent them scrambling to measure the piece inevitably to find it was off two thousandths of an inch. He identified various metals also by weight and feel. And no one could hide from him a repaired nick or scratch. It was a talent that bred legends.

Not all of Dad's time was spent working. He enjoyed social and civic affairs and spent many evenings during these years visiting with members of our large family of cousins. A number of years before, he was told he should get more exercise, so he began to take Arthur Murray dancing lessons at local studios in cities where he was traveling. Sometimes Mother went along, but I really enjoyed the dancing more than she did. My father taught me the intricate steps of the rumba and tango, as we danced so many evenings on the smooth floor of the basement to the music of phonograph records.

Before World War II, Dad walked about Hagerstown by himself, but by the late 1940s traffic had increased. The quiet cars of the day no longer gave him the audible signals which announced their presence. He had to give up his solo expeditions to town. Of course, for his business travels out of town he always had someone with him. Usually it was Horace Marlatt, but occasionally it was an associate from the factory.

152

# Perfect Circle Rings Go Into the Engines of America's Fighting Machines

## ON LAND . . . ON SEA . . . IN THE AIR

Into the machines of war—trucks, boats, tractors, tanks, and planes go Perfect Circle rings. Thousands and thousands of these rings are helping—and helping in a vital way—to put the "squeeze on the Japanese."

Our battle is production—production of rings to keep the war machines of America—and her Allies—rolling on land, on sea, and in the air. Where do Perfect Circles go—exactly? Look at the array of engines and machines below! They're typical.

(1) Perfect Circle rings go into the 1700 h.p. Wright Cyclone engine of this Curtiss dive bomber and into the Wright engine of the mammoth Boeing Flying Fortress (2)—planes which help to spell an Allies Victory.

The Douglas Attack Bomber (3) is propelled by six 1200 to 1600 h.p. P. C. equipped engines and the Douglas 8A-5 Bomber (4) is also equipped with the rings you Perfect Circle people make.

P. C. rings are regular equipment in the motors of the "fighting" International trucks (5)—one of many land machines with Perfect Circles.

(6) Here's a rear view of one of the famous Cyclone motors. Sure, it has P. C. rings, just like the speedy pursuit ship (7).

Our rings do their part in the motors of the big Half-Trac White Motor Company Scout Cars (8). These armored Personnel Carriers are capable of seating 14 men including the driver.

Allison aircraft engines (9) are keeping American planes flying. They're also on the Perfect Circle "In the Air" list.

The 33 foot Eureka landing boat (10) is propelled by a powerful and reliable P. C. equipped direct-drive 250 h.p. Hall-Scott "Invader" engine.

Heavy 155 millimeter guns are pulled by these International Trac-TracTors (11). Perfect Circles are in their motors.

*Important wartime customers of Perfect Circle were leaders in defense contracts with the United States.*

*During a World War II scrap drive, Ralph Teetor donated six airplane motors to the Cause for Victory. Pictured are interested New Castle spectators examining the motors while they were on display. The motors were from various countries, as their names signified — Damelier-Benz, LaRhone, Hispaño, Mercedes, Liberty, and Fiat. (Courtesy of The Victory Circle, the Perfect Circle employee newsletter, as it was called during the war.)*

*Ralph Teetor about 1942.*

*Nellie Teetor about 1942.*

*Shortly after Wendell Willkie was defeated for president of the United States Ralph gave a dinner party for Willkie in Ralph's home in 1941. Willkie, Ralph, John Warner, executive director of SAE.*

*Society of Automotive Engineers associates: Arthur Nutt, vice-president engineering of Wright Aeronautical Corp., Ralph, Henry Ford, John Warner. Nutt was president of SAE in 1940. At this occasion Ford was presented a lifetime membership in SAE.*

*The Main Street of Hagerstown, Indiana, in 1946. The population had grown to nearly two thousand. (Courtesy of The Circle magazine)*

# Tinkering Pays Off

My father spent the beginning of the fifties trying to convince me that I should finish my college education before I got married. It was a tough sell; I was in love and impatient. John Meyer had served in the Navy during World War II, graduated from college, and had a good job, so I saw no point in waiting around Northwestern where I was studying. We compromised. I stayed longer in Evanston than I intended, but didn't finish my degree until a number of years later.

For the summer of 1951, I decided to get a real job. I wanted it to be almost anyplace except Perfect Circle, but with business slow in most industries that summer, area employment offices took one look at my name and knew someone else needed the job more that I did. On the other hand, Perfect Circle's business was exceptionally strong and my father offered me a job in the chemistry lab at the foundry in New Castle. "I'll do it if you tell Red Fromuth (plant manager) to fire me if I don't do a good job," I replied. I really didn't have any choice. Besides, chemistry was my major and the lab sounded like a lot of fun.

It was fun. And I probably scored a few public relations points for management too, because I ended the summer with many friends among the employees. One production worker exclaimed to me in a surprised voice, "You are just like one of us!" She couldn't have said anything that would have pleased me more.

One day the project chemist, who was my boss, and I were conducting some new tests that released a cyanide gas. It was a particularly hot day and there was no air-conditioning, although there was a hood that was probably adequate for exhausting fumes . That evening I had a headache, cause unknown. At home I mentioned the cyanide process to my father and, with my usual drama, I speculated it that could have contributed to the headache. Shortly after, my father was on the phone. I didn't hear what he said, but the next day when I arrived at work just before eight in the morning, the wall beside the hood had been knocked out and a new, more powerful exhaust system was being installed. I was mortified. Fortunately only Red Fromuth knew who had ordered the change and he kept my secret.

On May 3, 1952, John Meyer and I were married in a lovely wedding at home. My parents were understandably disappointed that I didn't finish college before I was married, but, good sports that they were, they loyally supported my decision. Two days later they left for a short vacation, the first time they had ever flown together on the same airplane. They felt I had someone else to take care of me now.

For many years, Perfect Circle engineers had experimented with methods to centrifugally cast piston rings. They planned to slice the rings from "sleeves" or cylinders cast in spinning molds. But the spinning process caused the impurities in the iron to collect on the outside edge, while the purest, best material and smoothest finish was found on the inside surfaces. This result was the opposite of what was desired for making piston rings, where the working edge was the outside edge. After twelve years of experimental research, a few rings were successfully cast centrifugally, but the economic usefulness of the process had been limited. However, the engineers did discover that centrifugal casting was an excellent method for making cylinder sleeves, since the inside of that engine part was the critical surface. Centrifugally-cast sleeves quickly became an important Perfect Circle product.

Ralph found the process of centrifugal casting intriguing and wondered what other tasks such a process might perform. Why not make concrete blocks this way? Such a method should produce blocks with accurate and uniform dimensions. Their high density would produce increased strength and a smooth exterior surface. Since most of the water would be extracted from the cement as it spun, the shrinkage would be uniform as the block cured and not vary with the amount of water in the mix. Of course other shapes could also be molded by this method with the same advantages.

Ralph had plans drawn and a machine made to centrifugally cast concrete blocks. Results were disappointing. The concrete mixture spun out more than just water. The solid mixture had a tendency to become completely "unmixed" and separate into its original components of sand, lime, and water. Working a couple of years in some of his "spare" time, Ralph finally got a few good blocks and called upon his friend and patent attorney, Harry Lindsey, to apply for a patent in November, 1949. But a similar patent had been filed from England just a few months before. It didn't really matter. The concrete blocks Ralph was making weren't economically practical. They would cost three times more than conventional blocks. Besides, Ralph was onto something else really big now.

When Ralph was president of the Society of Automotive Engineers in 1936, the job brought him in contact with engineers from all over the world. As those creative people compared their concerns and hopes and dreams, it became apparent that improving the safety of automobiles was becoming a more and more compelling need. Up to this time power, speed, comfort, reliability, economy, and convenience had been driving the engineering research. Power and speed, especially, had developed beyond a driver's needs or ability to control on the narrow, winding roads that were still the norm in most sections of the country. Terrible accidents were the inevitable result as drivers indulged in their need for thrills at the expense of safety. Speed limits were imposed in many areas, but in just as many places they were soon violated. Safety, then, was a major theme in Ralph's speeches to his fellow engineers around the country in 1936. Ralph, correctly but somewhat naively, believed that safety was mainly the responsibility of the driver rather than the car manufacturer. Because all drivers wanted to be safe, he believed, education alone should solve the problem. Only if education did not result in safer driving should manufacturers consider mechanically limiting the speed which their cars could be driven.

But speed did continue to increase and so did accidents. As the fifties began, many trucking companies put speed governors on their fleets of trucks, effectively limiting the speed that those trucks could be driven on the highways. These proved to be not only irritating but sometimes dangerous. Occasionally drivers needed an extra burst of speed to pass another car or avoid some other hazard, and the governors did not allow for such flexibility. It became apparent that mechanically capping speed was not a satisfactory answer.

Meanwhile Ralph had the opportunity to ride in cars driven by many different types of drivers. Horace drove smoothly at a steady pace. Others were fast and jerky or slow and cautious. But Ralph jovially exclaimed that he might never have carried the speed control project any further if it hadn't been for his friend and patent attorney, Harry Lindsey, who was the jerkiest driver with whom he had ever ridden. For the next ten years Ralph thought about all this, creating and testing various ideas as he "tinkered" in his basement workshop. His inventive tinkering this time was not producing a fishing pole or concrete block. This new idea became one of today's most popular and useful automotive accessories—cruise control.

During World War II a national speed limit of thirty-five miles per hour was ordered by the government to conserve gasoline and rubber tires. Most motorists found it difficult and boring to travel long distances at such a slow speed. They complained that they had to watch their speedometers closely to keep from unconsciously accelerating to a higher speed. Ralph marveled at the small amount of additional time that it took to travel moderate distances at the lower speed. The limit added only about ten minutes to the sixty mile trip from Hagerstown to Indianapolis. He concluded that most drivers really didn't maintain higher speeds for very long at a time but frequently would slow down and speed up, wasting gasoline and endangering themselves and their passengers. Alternatively they were taking their eyes off the road frequently to check their speed on the speedometer.

What evolved in Ralph's mind was a speed control which the driver could set, using a dial on the dashboard, for any speed he wished to drive. When he reached his preset speed, he would feel a resisting pressure under the accelerator, against which he could hold his foot to steadily maintain his chosen speed uphill and downhill. If a burst of greater speed was needed, he could consciously press through the resistance on the accelerator. There was no lock-in; the driver's foot exerted the pressure. When the car slowed back to the speed he had set, he could again ride the pressure, knowing he was traveling his chosen speed without looking at the speedometer. Ralph had discovered a method that would allow for smooth, consistent speed control without having to dangerously cap the speed of a vehicle. The driver could keep his eyes on the road, and maintain his responsibility for adhering to a safe speed. This first speed control was powered by a vacuum from the manifold.

Ralph filed for the first patent on his device in spring of 1945, while it was still a basement workshop tinkering project. He later jokingly said that when he became the president of Perfect Circle in 1947, he didn't have enough to do so he began working more on the speed control. There may have been more than a grain of truth to this; the many ceremonial duties required of him possibly gave him some extra time to think about it.

To help with this project, he hired Woody Ulrich, the boy who had won the boat race for the Scout uniform years before. A Perfect Circle employee for many years, Woody started working with Ralph two evenings a week in a little machine shop across the street from Ralph's house. Woody made the drawings and blueprints needed for the mechanics to make the parts and later did the drawings for the patents. Most of the parts were made right there in the shop but a few had to be purchased from outside suppliers. Ralph and Woody traveled to the Woodward Governor Company in Rockford, Illinois, several times for repeated revisions of a special conical spring. Driving most of the day, they typically arrived in the evening with the prints. Then the Woodward engineers worked far into the night making the spring to the new specifications, to have it ready for Ralph and Woody to take back with them the next day.

The first few prototypes of the speed control were large and cumbersome, more than a foot long and several inches in diameter. It was a wonder Ralph could find room for one under the hood, but he soon had it operating on his own Buick. (Ironically, Buick was the only division of General Motors which did not become a customer of the speed control years later.) Gradually he and Woody refined the device until it was smaller and simpler, improving the performance and lowering the cost.

For some of this development Ralph bought a 1948 Oldsmobile, which he kept at the house. There were times when the men didn't need to work on it, and I was allowed to drive it, a reprieve from my assigned seven-passenger Cadillac. I loved that little car. One day when I was driving the Olds with my friends, the speedometer was disconnected, waiting for installation of a new speed control. With no speedometer to tell me that I was going too fast, I sailed over the hilly country roads as fast as I dared, jouncing and frightening everyone but me. As I look back on that now, I realize how blessed I was that day. I deserved less.

By 1949 Ralph had a pretty good working model, but more development was needed to prepare it for production. Then too, the "new baby" needed a name. Records of copyright searches show serious consideration was given to "Controlmatic," "Touchomatic," "Prestomatic," and "Pressomatic." Nellie suggested the winning label, "Speedostat," and so it was to be. It would be called simply the "Stat" at home and customers could apply their own trade names.

Who would manufacture this new device? Believing that it could grow into something important, Ralph very much wanted Perfect Circle to take it on. Besides, that way he could continue to oversee it. But his cousins on the board of directors voted "no" to the new product. That was a setback he had not anticipated, and he was sincerely disappointed.

Briefly Ralph toyed with the idea of manufacturing the Speedostat himself. Fortunately his better judgment prevailed and he searched the automotive field. Since he was so widely acquainted in the automotive parts business, before long he had struck a deal with Pierce Governor in Anderson, Indiana. The contract signed in late 1953 gave the company exclusive rights to manufacture and sell the Speedostat in return for a five percent royalty to Ralph. The next year Ralph was asked to serve on the board of directors of Pierce Governor. The January, 1954, issue of *Popular Science Monthly*

carried a four-page description of the Speedostat and how it worked—
even though it was still a long way from being ready for production.
The first national advertising was exciting. They were finally getting
on with it— or so they thought.

Ralph joined the Pierce Governor Board on May 5, 1955. Minutes of that meeting reported glowing enthusiasm for projected sales
for the Speedostat in the truck market. Ford was testing it and
General Motors Truck and Coach, International Harvester, Chevrolet,
and Dodge had all shown interest. Pierce had no plans for promoting
the Stat in passenger cars until it had "conquered its place in the
truck field." But in the months that followed nothing happened. Following the magazine publicity, a few handmade samples were sent to
companies who requested them, but Pierce provided no follow-up and
enthusiasm died. Nor did Pierce prepare for production. While the
cause of this was never explained, it appears to have been a combination of poor management and internal financial problems at
Pierce Governor. Finally, at the end of 1955, Ralph canceled the contract with Pierce Governor and resigned from the Board of Directors.

Ralph was presented with another problem in 1955 which probably prevented his deeper involvement with Pierce Governor at such
a crucial time. The UAW-CIO struck Perfect Circle again. The strike
was part of a carefully planned pressure campaign within the automobile industry. Each year the union would select one of the large automobile companies for a major strike to push through demands, knowing that if, for instance, Ford gave in, General Motors and Chrysler
would feel compelled to follow. To Ralph's dismay this strategy had
been successfully used to gain the union shop for all the automotive
manufacturers. Now the union was pressing the parts suppliers for the
same concessions.

After the test strike in 1948, the union knew that Perfect Circle
was a stronghold for the right-to-work philosophy, and a vigorous pro-
ponent of right-to-work legislation in the Indiana legislature. If
Perfect Circle could be forced to accept union shop, many other companies would capitulate more easily. The UAW-CIO badly misjudged
their adversary. Not only was the president of Perfect Circle the most
stubborn German they had probably ever crossed, with the rest of

management staunchly with him to the death, but most of the employees were just as stubbornly loyal and independent as their leaders.

The strike began on July 25 at Perfect Circle's plants in New Castle, Hagerstown, Richmond, and Tipton. Most of the employees continued to work through the picket lines the union set up, and at first the company was not drastically disrupted. After giving the back fences of Hagerstown an overdose of gossip and rumor, things were settling down by early October. Then the union announced it would turn up the heat. That same evening, Ralph and Nellie were walking the seven blocks home from visiting Ralph's ninety-year-old mother, Kate, when a parade of cars appeared on Main Street coming in from New Castle. They were strikers the union was bringing in from other towns for a big demonstration the next day. Both Ralph and Nellie and the cars arrived at the same time at the corner where a neighborhood gas station was located. The Teetors stopped, of course, because they needed to cross the street, while the strikers turned the corner around them to go to the factory. Some of the strikers recognized who they were and began cutting through the gas station with much jeering and yelling, effectively marooning them on a little corner of sidewalk with no way to escape. The company president and his wife were trapped for about fifteen minutes, although it must have seemed much longer. Ralph later declared that he wasn't frightened, because he just didn't believe they would hurt them. In light of future developments, he may have been a bit naive.

The next morning the crowds were in front of the factory preventing anyone from entering. Of course, a number of the management personnel had spent the night inside the plant. The local employees mostly stayed away that day. So complete was the "outsider" presence at the plant that when the president of the local chapter of the union tried to get through the mob, he couldn't do it because no one recognized him. The personnel manager inside the plant was called out to identify the man.

The lieutenant governor finally sent in the National Guard to restore order after gun shots, harassment and vandalism had turned the scene ugly and dangerous. By the time it was settled, this strike would be considered the most violent in Indiana history and one of the worst in the country. Most of the violence occurred at the New Castle foundry. That chaotic scene was dramatically pictured in the October 17, 1955, issue of *Life* magazine. The evening that *Life* hit the newsstands Nellie and Ralph were eating supper at the local restaurant while Nellie read aloud to Ralph the sensationalized article accompanying the pictures.

> *An Indiana city last week exploded with the kind of bloody labor battle whose ugly look the U.S. had almost forgotten. Inside the Perfect Circle piston ring foundry at New Castle (pop. 18,271), some 120 nonstriking workers and officials armed with pistols, rifles and shotguns watched 1,200 members of the United Auto Workers marching to shut down the plant. Shots rang out from the factory. The march stopped and then answering shots whistled from beyond the plant fence. Before the volleys ended, seven men and a woman were wounded.*
>
> *The trouble had been building up ever since the union struck the foundry and three other Perfect Circle plants in July. The union's key demand was for a union shop to replace the present contract's open shop. It also wanted negotiations at New Castle to cover all four plants. But the company, aware that weak locals at the other three plants were weakened by worker dissension, insisted that each plant negotiate separately.*
>
> *When the strike began, the Perfect Circle foundry at New Castle shut down. But the company, a family concern headed by Ralph Teetor, an uncompromising, totally blind engineer, used nonstrikers to keep operations going elsewhere. After mass picketing was barred, the New Castle foundry was reopened. Nonstrikers were beaten up, and company officials stored arms in the plant. When 35 strikers, including the president of the New Castle local, were fired violence was set off . . .*

At this point in the narrative Ralph turned to Nellie and declared, "Nellie, I just don't know how you have put up with such a terrible man for a husband all these years." Several of their fellow diners nearby joined in their laughter. The back fences in Hagerstown were buzzing again.

*The Dayton Daily News* gave a more balanced view of the incident and of Ralph's part in it.

*There had been no violence in previous strikes. The present walkout began after the union presented the company with a five-point demand calling for a union shop, arbitration of grievances, wage increases, improved pensions, and layoff pay.*

*"We have always gotten along well with the union," Teetor said, "until this year when instead of bargaining they laid down a list of demands and told us we would have to grant them or else." The company, he said, is unalterably opposed to the union shop which would force union membership on its employees.*

*"We will fight that principle to the end," Teetor said. "Things are different down here. I know everybody in Hagerstown and everybody knows me.*

*"Three of my closest neighbors work on a production line in our plant. You just don't force people to join unions here like you do in the big city. If the union can persuade them to join, that's something else again."*

What did the employees think? One of the engineers who was in Richmond at the time said, "I had a double barreled shotgun, a twenty-two rifle and a thirty-eight pistol, and I was ready to die for the cause of open shop. It was a religious thing! It was free enterprise. I don't know, you got real emotional about the thing."

Safety director Bob Beeson remembered that with constant threats of the strikers to blow up the plant, the men inside the plant were prepared to defend the Hagerstown plant too. He said, "We couldn't get out of the factory for five days but the mail always came through so my wife mailed me clean underwear." Others had sad stories of harassment of their families and damage to their homes.

By the end of November, elections were held and, except for New Castle, the UAW-CIO was voted out of all the struck plants where associations of local employees were established. The strike was settled on exactly the same terms that Perfect Circle offered before it began. The back fences became quiet once more and Ralph went back to work on the Stat.

He felt the need to speed preparing the device for production to make up for the delay at Pierce Governor and the strike. He added Dick Fleischhaur, a friend and toolmaker who had just retired from Perfect Circle, to the team. He also added a few machines to the equipment in the little building where the men were working.

On one occasion Ralph asked Luther Parsons, tool room superintendent, to accompany him to the Cincinnati Milling Machine Company to purchase a new milling machine. Horace drove them to Cincinnati. As Luther described the event, "The sales manager showed us all around the plant. Ralph walked with him and Horace and I tagged along behind." Ralph always walked with his hand lightly on the upper arm of the person guiding him. "They came to a pair of swinging glass doors and one was standing open. The sales manager, forgetting that Ralph couldn't see, walked through the door that was open, allowing Ralph to walk right into the closed door beside it. A huge bump raised on Ralph's forehead. But he never lost his temper. I would have! We walked right on and finished up our business and he even bought a milling machine that day. You know it had to hurt but he never complained."

Much of Dick and Woody's time was spent keeping up with Ralph's improvements in the Stat. Information they had received from the testing by Pierce Governor gave the clear message that customers wanted a "lock in" feature which would maintain the selected speed while permitting the driver to take his foot off of the accelerator.

Ralph knew that the Stat could be made to hold the speed. Always concerned about safety, though, he had resisted adding that feature. What if the driver became distracted, panicky, or fell asleep? His concerns were unfounded. Extensive road-testing demonstrated that this automatic throttle was quite safe. Because customers continued to clamor for it, Ralph engineered a small electric motor into the Stat. This control would hold the speed magnetically until the driver touched the brake pedal, immediately disengaging the speed control. Although more expensive than the vacuum method he had used for the first Speedostat models, he was confident that this automatic throttle would not fail to disengage.

The Speedostat was a new idea for a passenger car. No one could reliably predict how many people would really order such a device.

As with most new accessories, car owners felt no need for something they had never tried and had survived very well without. There was, obviously, a big selling job ahead. While Ralph did explore the possibility of manufacturing the Stat with several of his friends in other companies such as Borg Warner and Delco-Remy Division of General Motors, more than ever he wanted Perfect Circle to manufacture the Speedostat. This time he had an important ally.

Bill Prosser was first hired by Dan Teetor in Tipton and came to Hagerstown with him when Dan's firm merged with Perfect Circle. During Bill's pre-employment interview, Dan asked him what job he would like to have. Bill answered, "Eventually I'd like to be president."

Thirty years later he was nearing his goal. As a capable general manager, he was relieving Ralph of some of the responsibilities of the presidency so he could work on the Speedostat. Bill wanted the Speedostat for Perfect Circle. The many improvements Perfect Circle had engineered into piston rings now meant this basic product was far more durable and rarely had to be replaced in automobile engines. It appeared that piston rings were nearing the limit of efficiency and durability—and replacement sales potential too. To grow and remain prosperous Perfect Circle needed new products. Bill finally convinced Ralph's still reluctant cousins that the Speedostat presented a good opportunity, and on March 1, 1957, Perfect Circle bought the patents for fifty thousand dollars. Ralph was delighted. Now he could begin selling the Stat in Detroit for his company. He had a wonderful new product and he still had enough old friends in the motor city to make selling it fun.

With no regrets, Ralph resigned his position as president of Perfect Circle to become chief engineer and direct the Speedostat team. Bill Prosser was elected president of Perfect Circle, fulfilling his career-long ambition.

There was work to be done. The Speedostat had to be engineered separately for each model of car. Nothing yet was ready for production, a very different activity than producing the handmade prototypes used in demonstrations. Sourcing supplies, building production equipment, and training employees remained to be done. And, of course, everything was dependent on advertising and sales.

Now that the company was committed, Perfect Circle moved rapidly. Woody was reassigned to devote his full time to the project. Unforeseen difficulties arose when, the next day, Woody was called to jury duty for six months on a week by week call-in basis. As it turned out, he was called to serve only a week or two, but with the uncertainty of his attendance, an additional engineer, Earl Daggy, was assigned to the Stat project too. Herman Teetor led the advertising department in an all-out blitz of press releases, which were given prominent display all around the country from *The San Francisco Chronicle* to *The New York Times* and even in Europe. Articles nearly always included a picture of Bill Prosser and Ralph peering under the hood of a car admiring the new device. Congratulations and inquiries poured in.

The small machine shop that Ralph and Woody had been using for engineering was inadequate for the expanded activity of Speedostat, so Ralph built a larger building next door to it. It would be a few years before Speedostat engineering relocated within the Perfect Circle walls.

As they went into production, Ralph's perennial perfectionism caused frustration among the engineers and customers. "He never stopped changing it." Woody related. "We would just get the Stat ready for production when Ralph would come in with a new idea to change something. I would tell him that it looked like a good idea but I didn't think we could afford it." Woody was used to having to work within a budget. Ralph didn't care about a budget. "Oh, that's okay," Ralph would reply, "I'll pay for it."

Whether he paid for the changes or not, he usually got his way. Ralph's first priority was making the Stat perfect—the other men were charged with getting it into production.

Tall, blond, Gene Stohler transferred from piston ring sales to sell the Stat to the car manufacturers. He travelled with Ralph and/or Woody to Detroit to meet with the automobile companies. Gene related his first trip with amusement. He drove a Speedostat-equipped car to meet Ralph and Bill Prosser at the Book Cadillac Hotel in downtown Detroit. It was his first time driving into the city and he finally arrived at Ralph and Bill's hotel room just before dinner. Bill quickly told Gene that he was sorry but, because of a change in plans, he had to leave immediately to return home, and Gene would be staying with Ralph that night. Gene replied, "I don't know what I'm supposed to do! I don't know how to take care of Ralph because he doesn't see."

Bill replied, "Don't worry about it. He'll take care of you."

Gene affirmed that was exactly what happened. Ralph asked, "Gene, what would you like for dinner?" Gene, of course, answered that he would like whatever Ralph preferred. "How about a good steak and some American fried potatoes?" Ralph suggested.

"That would be wonderful," Gene agreed.

"Fine, we'll go to Berman's," Ralph decided. Putting on their coats, they went down to the front door of the hotel. Gene started to hail a cab.

"No, we can walk," Ralph suggested.

"Gosh, Ralph, I don't know how to get there. I don't even know where I am!" Gene objected

"That's okay, I'll show you," was Ralph's reply. Turning left out of the hotel they walked about two blocks, turned left again and went around behind the bus station to the restaurant. "I would defy a sighted person to find that restaurant!" Gene declared later.

After a good dinner Ralph asked Gene if he would like some ice cream. "Why don't we have a Saunders' hot fudge sundae?" Gene signaled the waiter. "No. We'll walk there," Ralph insisted.

The Saunders ice cream parlor was about six blocks away, over on Woodward Avenue. "I never felt so helpless in my life," Gene commented later. " After we walked quite a distance I looked up and down the street and said, 'Ralph I don't see any restaurant or ice cream shop called Saunders along here.' "

"What is that up to your right?" Ralph asked. There it was with the sign hidden, right where Ralph said it would be.

This type of story about Ralph can be duplicated by nearly everyone who knew him well. Whether it was a favorite restaurant in Chicago or New York, an ice cream parlor in Philadelphia or a candy store in Cannes, France, if Ralph had enjoyed something there he could probably find the place again. He admitted to Gene that he counted his steps. But he was also known to give directions in a car by taking clues from railroad crossings and curves. Gene admitted to accusing Ralph of faking blindness. "I know you can really see," he teased. Ralph laughed.

Gene marveled at the success Ralph had in getting the attention and sympathetic ear of almost anyone in Detroit with whom he wanted to meet. Of course many of his old engineering friends were now in top positions of responsibility. Ed Cole was president of General Motors. Ed and Ralph met many times during those years, spending hours discussing such topics as whether the Wankel rotary engine was ever going to become workable. Ralph didn't think the Wankel would succeed, even though General Motors was putting a great deal of effort into developing it at the time. They talked about politics, business concerns and whatever was new in the engineering field. The kinship Ralph felt with automobile industry heads did not extend to Henry Ford. Ralph and Henry Ford were acquainted through SAE and NAM, but though Ralph and Gene tried on many occasions to meet with Mr. Ford to show him the Speedostat, they never were granted an appointment with him personally. The Ford Company, however, did eventually purchase the Stat for installation in their cars.

According to those who traveled with Ralph, he was quite clever about getting to see the person he really needed to meet. If they were turned away by one executive, Ralph told Gene or Woody, "There is someone else in this organization that we need to find." He always knew someone else, usually higher in the organization, to ask for. Or he would call one of his friends to ask them who to talk with about the speed control. Frequently that person would call in the man they had tried to meet in the first place. "And it doesn't hurt anything if they feel just a bit sorry for you either," Ralph once admitted to Gene with a grin. His "inconvenience" could sometimes be conveniently useful.

Many years later Dixon Speas, president of Aviation Consulting, Inc., related, "One of my most memorable visits with Ralph was the day I introduced him to Igor Sikorsky in Detroit at an SAE meeting. The two were obviously completely enthralled with each other's professional achievements. I remember that they both confessed that they were avid readers of *Popular Mechanics*. Both were absolute masters in developing ideas into practical reality."

Early one morning in Detroit Gene and Ralph were the only ones in the coffee shop of the hotel when Ralph said, "Shhh, listen. Boss Kettering is in here."

Gene looked around. "Ralph, there isn't one soul in this breakfast room except you and me," Gene replied.

Soon Ralph said, "Just a minute!" Just then they heard a faint, high-pitched laugh. "That's Boss Kettering and I knew he was in this room, I just knew it. Now let's go see him!" he exclaimed.

Gene puzzled, "I don't know where he is, Ralph. I can't see anyone."

When the maître d' was called over, he explained that indeed Kettering was sitting in a little alcove behind a screen. Learning that Ralph was there, Kettering joined the two men for breakfast and a friendly chat.

By late 1957 Ford, Chevrolet and Chrysler were all testing the Speedostat. Chrysler, however, was the first to commit, offering it on their 1958 Imperial, New Yorker and Windsor models. It proved to be so popular that by the end of 1958 they were offering it on their entire line of new cars. They decided to market it with the name, "Auto Pilot." They insisted that it have the added lock-in feature which would hold the car at the selected speed when the driver took his foot off the accelerator.

The next year Cadillac came on board, offering the Speedostat as optional equipment on all its new cars. Cadillac chose to call it "Cruise Control." Ralph was happy to be selling to Cadillac again. He felt most at home there. But he was not much impressed with the name "Cruise Control." He didn't think it was a name that would ever become popular. Fortunately Ralph was too busy engineering the Stat to worry about it.

For the past few years the government, too, had been eyeing the accident statistics, and some of the states, as well as the federal government, were looking for opportunities to address the safety issues. The leading proposal of the federal government involved requiring car manufacturers to limit the speed by installing a governor. The automobile companies, of course, opposed the idea because they knew that a governor would be unacceptable to their customers. Ralph wrote letters to every congressman pointing out that not only would a speed governor fail to solve the problem of speed, it added the danger of inflexibility to meet a crisis. A house highway safety committee visited Ford, General Motors, and Chrysler. According to Robert Lienert, writing for *Automotive News*, GM impressed the lawmakers with the extensive engineering and testing they were undertaking to build maximum safety into their cars. Engineering vice-president, Charles Chayne, then reminded the congressmen, "In high-speed crashes passenger protection admittedly becomes more difficult and any spectacular accomplishment in protecting car occupants can be achieved only by repealing the natural physical laws of motion and energy." He too argued convincingly that limiting the speed of the car or its horsepower added more danger to the passengers rather than less.

As information on the new Speedostat became widely known, critical concern again was expressed about the safety of the lock-in feature. A number of people, none of whom had ever driven with the Stat, insisted that this must be a dangerous feature. The first to respond to this concern was Senator Arthur Mullen of the Massachusetts legislature. In February, 1959, Senator Mullen was promoting SB. 136, "An Act Prohibiting the Operation of a Motor Vehicle Equipped With a Constant Speed Lock or Device." Interviewed by a Perfect Circle salesman, he insisted he was only concerned with the "safety factor" and that no commercial interest was being represented. He admitted he knew nothing of how the Speedostat worked or other similar devices now being marketed. Furthermore, he didn't really think his bill would pass. Before Perfect Circle had an opportunity to offer him a demonstration, he died of a heart attack and no one else in the Massachusetts legislature took up the cause. Following that threat, Perfect Circle took great care to familiarize state police, state highway safety committees, governors and anyone else who would listen with the safety features of the Stat. They could demonstrate that it was engineered in such a way that it absolutely could not fail to disengage. When a driver is confronted with danger, Perfect Circle reminded the legislators, the normal reaction is always to hit the brake which, when the Stat is operating, disengages the speed control. In all of the automobile personal injury or property damage lawsuits brought in the nearly forty years in which the Stat has been in use, not one award was made on the basis that the Stat malfunctioned or was at fault.

During those first years there were also a few doomsayers who were sure the lock-in feature would increase the monotony of driving and make the driver sleepy. Some alleged it might encourage distractions for the driver, or cause panic. A few newspaper writers tried to gain attention by publishing grave warnings about the Speedostat, but fast growing popularity and satisfactory customer experience soon dispelled concern.

By the time the strike of 1955 was settled and the concerns with Pierce Governor's handling of the Speedostat had been resolved, Nellie convinced Ralph that they both needed a vacation. Although Ralph never really thought he needed a vacation—he was always doing what he liked to do best—he readily agreed that a change would be welcome. They planned to embark on a Mediterranean cruise with George and Louise Keagy for three weeks in March, 1956, on the *Constitution,* a United States Line cruise ship offering fancy trappings and many ports of call. In this era when "proper dress" called for hats and gloves for the ladies and white shirts and ties for the men, when "dressing for dinner" twice a week on the ship meant tuxedos and long dresses, the proposed trip called for a large wardrobe. Ralph hated to carry many suitcases. Wheeled luggage had not been thought of. What to do?

Nellie, always modestly but elegantly dressed, looked at what she had, organized it carefully, and packed two suitcases. Ralph thought about it for a couple of weeks, then invented a new suitfolder to fit into his two-suiter case. The case now would hold four suits without causing a wrinkle. His invention consisted of a double rectangular metal frame around which one folded the suits, all of which were secured with a piece of fabric and snaps. With four suits packed, there still was space in the same suitcase for four pairs of shoes, six shirts, socks, pajamas, underwear, and his toilet case. When Ralph displayed it, the suitfolder became the talk of his friends on the ship. After he returned home, of course, he had some ideas for improvement. Initially Nellie had sewn the fabric for him on her sewing machine. However, that soon ended. In perfecting this case, Ralph wanted the fabric to be sewn within a thirty-second of an inch of his measurements. Nellie sewed beautifully but didn't have the patience to achieve that degree of perfection. "You just can't sew fabric that exactly!" she objected.

"Why not?" was his patient reply.

"The fabric stretches," she informed him. Ralph remained unconvinced, but took the project to the engineers across the street. They prepared samples and drawings so Ralph's good friend Harry Lindsey could apply for a patent. Ralph may have intuitively known that some day there could be life without the Stat and he might need a new project. The suitcase insert provided much diversion, although it never became a financially successful product.

Ralph had a modest share of publicity. Another one of his fellow passengers had been a reporter who wrote for *The Rocky Mountain News*:

*I would like you to meet Ralph R. Teetor, one of the passengers on this cruise . . . He has participated in all the shore trips—including the two-day one to Rome. He has enjoyed every minute as much as anyone and more than most, and it strikes me he has seen more than the majority of the passengers.*

*What makes this all so unusual is that the world would call Teetor blind. He injured his eye with a knife when he was five years old, and the accident cost him his physical sight. I only wish I could see as much with two good eyes as he does with none.*

*With him, besides his wife, is a cousin, George Keagy and his wife. Keagy told me that he and his cousin had been playing together on that day when the one boy injured his eye . . .*

*I first began to notice Teetor out on the deck as we approached a port. He seemed to get the feel of the approaching city before any of the rest of us. He always faced carefully toward the approaching shore and skyline.*

*The reason you knew about his eyes was that, whenever he moved across the deck he touched the elbow of one of the members of his party.*

*I don't believe he missed a museum, a cathedral, or a palace. And I'd risk a small wager that he could describe them better than any other one among us.*

*Part of it, of course, is because Keagy and the others describe everything carefully for him and point out the things that shouldn't be missed. I saw him at the entrance to the Vatican library, where the huge dual one-way staircase winds between floors. A lot of visitors miss this unusual stairway, but Teetor didn't. After it had been described to him, I watched as he moved a few steps down the incline—carefully feeling the rail with his hand and the treads with his feet. Then he returned to the top. He had seen the spiral.*

*And it was on one particularly fine night, near the end of the cruise schedule, that several of us were sitting in a prom deck lounge enjoying the lecture. Teetor poked his head in from the deck outside. "Come on out," he called to some friends. "You must see this gorgeous moon tonight."*

In all of his travels, Dad typically carried a large amount of cash in the especially compartmentalized wallet which he tucked in his hip pocket. He didn't consider cash-carrying risky because he was sure his highly developed sense of touch and hearing would make it impossible to pick his pocket. A change of planes in the Miami Airport en route to Puerto Rico proved him wrong. Even the loss of over two thousand dollars was not as distressing to him as the blow to his pride: he hadn't detected the loss as it happened. After that, Mother always carried some traveler's checks.

*A typical scene with Ralph in his workshop any evening in the 1950s.*

*The inventor of this three-wheeled vehicle hoped Ralph or Perfect Circle would help him market it. They didn't, but Ralph enjoyed it one afternoon in 1951 in the Perfect Circle parking lot. (Courtesy of Don Beeson)*

*Ralph and Marjorie entering her wedding in their home May 3, 1952.*

*Ralph in a 1911 Ford with owner Herschel Shepler of Greenfield, Indiana, in front of Ralph's house, 1953.*

Bill Prosser and Ralph inspecting the new device for a publicity picture which Perfect Circle used for marketing the Speedostat, 1957.

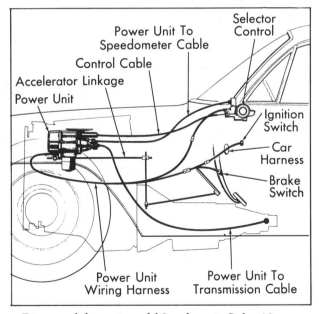

Diagram of electronic model Speedostat in Safety News, a publication of the National Safety Council in 1965.

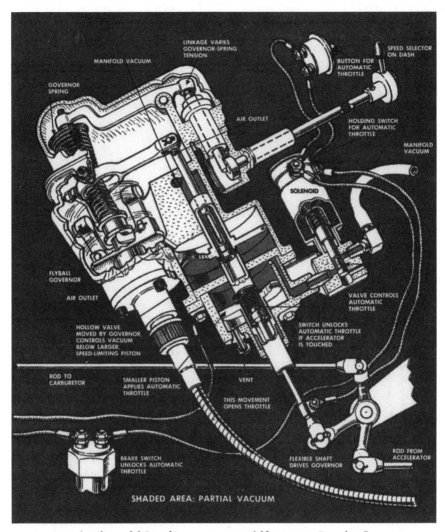

*Diagram of early model Speedostat using manifold vacuum*, Popular Science *magazine reprint of an article, January 1954.*

*Scenes from the big strike at Perfect Circle in 1955: crossing the picket line in Hagerstown.*

*Gathering for trouble at the main gate of the foundry in New Castle.*

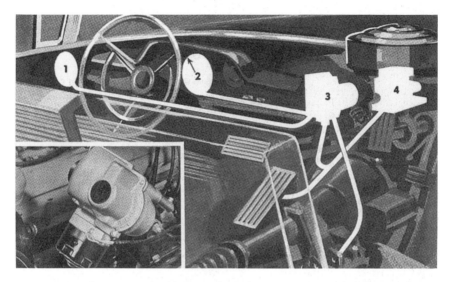

## Here's how the Perfect Circle Speed Control works

The speedometer (2) is driven indirectly from the transmission through the Speed Control (3) which is operated by an electric motor. The accelerator is connected to the carburetor (4) and the Speed Control is connected to the accelerator.

**WHEN USED AS A SPEED REMINDER,** the driver sets the control dial (1) at the legal limit and accelerates until he feels a gentle accelerator pedal resistance. This **exclusive** feature resists, but does not limit, a throttle opening greater than that required to maintain a pre-selected speed uphill, downhill or on the straightaway. Whenever this pedal resistance occurs, the driver knows he has reached the maximum speed he has set for himself. He never needs to check his speedometer. He may,

at any time, press past this resistance for immediate passing speed and power and the control remains in effect when the former speed is resumed.

**AS AN AUTOMATIC CRUISE CONTROL ON THE HIGHWAY OR TOLLWAY,** the driver makes a speed setting as before, accelerates until pedal resistance is felt, then touches the "cruising" button. Driver can take his foot off the accelerator because the Speed Control maintains the desired speed regardless of grade variations. Once again, instant passing speed is available by stepping on the accelerator to exceed the pre-set limit. The Speed Control is automatically disengaged when the brake pedal is touched. To re-engage, accelerate to the set speed and touch "cruising" button.

## Perfect Circle Speed Controls need no lubricating or adjusting

The Perfect Circle Speed Control is a compact, electrically-operated, self-contained unit that seldom, if ever, needs servicing. It requires no lubrication; there is no

fluid to replace, there are no vacuum lines to leak, no adjustments to make. It is solidly engineered for trouble-free performance and greater driving satisfaction.

### PERFECT CIRCLE CORPORATION
**Speedostat Division • Hagerstown, Indiana**

Form No. 2412 - 12-62 - 5M

Printed in U.S.A.

*A Perfect Circle Speed Control advertisement around 1963.*

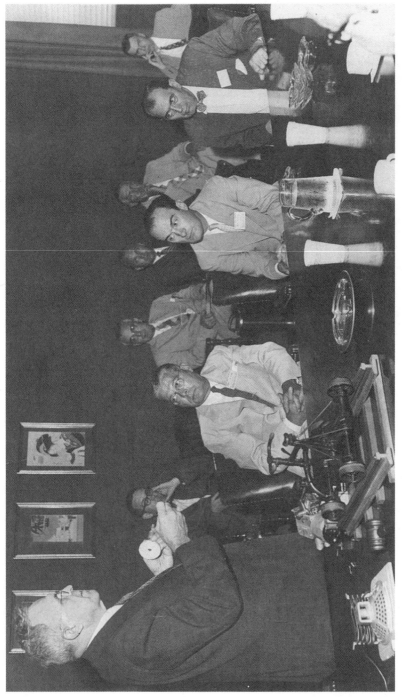

*Ralph demonstrates the speed control for Perfect Circle and Chrysler salesmen. Sitting against the wall are Woody Ulrich, second from right, and Gene Stohler, third from right.*

*The Perfect Circle Board of Directors, 1955. Clockwise (left to right) Herman Teetor, Dan Teetor, Blair Hartley, George Rea, company treasurer; Ralph, Lothair Teetor, Bill Prosser, Macy Teetor, George Keagy, Donald Teetor.*

# One More Round

The next few years were divided between selling the Speedostat in Detroit with Gene and Woody, and engineering it to fit each make or model of automobile that now wanted to offer it. With the popularity of the automatic throttle or "lock-in," Ralph worked to perfect the all-electronic version of the Speedostat. Chrysler and Cadillac were asking for an additional step, an automatic resume or re-lock-in which would function after the driver had touched the brake and then resumed speed. Ralph was as concerned for the safety of this feature as he had been for the automatic throttle itself. In fact, meeting with Chrysler engineers, he flatly refused to add this feature out of his concern for safety, even though he knew how to do it. Chrysler added the resume and, after extensive testing, it, too, proved to be safe and extremely popular. The custom engineering department which designed the Stat to fit individual cars moved its headquarters to the Perfect Circle factory. Ralph and several of the engineers, though, remained behind working on more improvements. Actual production of the Speedostat took place in the factory. In Ralph's workshop the hectic pace of the past few years could become a little more relaxed.

In 1959 Ralph hired Bob Morris, a fine craftsman and engineer, to make up new models of the Speedostat. Ralph would tell his new employee exactly how he wanted the new model to be made, then Bob drew up the plans on paper and made the model for Ralph to examine. "It took me a while to get used to making something that took two or three weeks to complete, get it all done just to the 'nth' degree and then have him look at it for a few minutes and just toss it in the waste basket. He already had another idea," Bob said.

At this early phase in the Stat's production, the car manufacturers were buying the Speedostat, but they were also clamoring to have it engineered simpler and cheaper. "They couldn't build a car that would last long enough to justify the quality that Ralph had put into the Stat," Bob commented. When Ralph hired Bob, they agreed to a one-year contract. Bob stayed for the rest of Ralph's lifetime.

During the winter of 1957–58, Earlham College was looking for a new president to replace President Thomas Jones, who was retiring. Ralph was on the search committee. The candidate he preferred for the position was Landrum Bolling, formerly an international news reporter in Europe during World War II and now a professor at Earlham. Ralph saw in him the leadership and human relations skills which, combined with the Christian love and integrity he had developed as a Quaker, would serve the college well. Indeed, these qualities would eventually carry Landrum Bolling into the powerful role of an internationally trusted reconciliation agent in the Middle East. Now Ralph's choice prevailed and he was asked to inform Landrum that he had been chosen to be president of Earlham. "That's wonderful!" replied Landrum, who would take office in midsummer 1958.

In the meantime, the Friends' overseas education missions' office asked Landrum to visit Kenya to develop an American-style comprehensive high school, combining academics with vocational training in carpentry, agriculture, and other manual arts. Former President Jones and Landrum wanted Earlham to help with this project but had no money in the budget for travel to Africa.

"That will be fine," said Ralph, "I will give you the money to go to Africa if you will then meet Nellie and me to travel for a few weeks around Europe." Ralph and Nellie had wanted to return to Europe independently but were apprehensive about making the trip without someone along with them who knew his way about.

It was agreed. In late March Landrum left for Kenya and Ralph, Nellie, and Francis Bolling, Landrum's wife, boarded the USS *United States* for Le Havre, France. As they parted, Nellie's last words rang in

Landrum's ears: "Whatever you do, Landrum, be there when the boat comes in." He assured her he would.

Landrum left Nairobi, Kenya, two days early to fulfill his promise. After changing planes in Cairo, as the connecting flight took off, he knew something was seriously wrong. One of the four engines had failed. After landing back in Cairo, he learned that his plane would not leave until the following night. He reboarded at the appointed time only to find the same thing happening to another engine. Realizing now that he could not be at the dock in Le Havre in time to meet the ship, he cabled Ralph and Nellie on the ship, instructing them to take a taxi to the hotel in Paris where he would meet them. The cable never reached them.

Landrum finally reached Rome, the next stop on his journey, where he bought a *New York Herald Tribune*. As he casually leafed through the paper he discovered a large notice advising that, due to severe storms at sea, the *USS United States* would be twenty-four hours late arriving at Le Havre. "Wonderful! I can still make it!" exclaimed Landrum. He flew to Paris and checked into the hotel, where he learned that the first train to Le Havre would leave early the next morning. Ralph, Nellie, and Francis got off the boat, had their luggage loaded into Ralph's Buick which had come on the boat with them, and were about to pull away from the gas pump when Landrum's taxi drove up beside them. They could not have met more precisely no matter how well they had planned.

One of the most memorable experiences of the trip for Ralph and Nellie was a dinner in Vienna with a friend of Landrum's. Gustav Herzog was a half-Jewish Viennese journalist who worked for the Associated Press Bureau in Vienna at the beginning of the German occupation of Austria. According to Landrum, Herzog saw the terrible atrocities that the Germans were committing in Austria as they overpowered his country, and he reported the truth to his American boss at the Associated Press. The publishing of the information in the free world so infuriated the Nazis that they pressed to find out who was to blame. They traced the leakage to Herzog and arrested him. He spent the next seven years in Auschwitz and Buchenwald but he survived. "He was skin and bones when I first met him at the end of

World War II, just a few weeks out of prison and looking for a job," Landrum reported to Ralph and Nellie. "His Christian wife and mother-in-law had survived but they had no money and very little food. His Jewish mother had been raped by the Russians following the German invasion, and she was dying of syphilis." The two couples heard stories of the difficulties of life in Austria and Germany after the war ended. Only with the help of Landrum, then a war correspondent in United States uniform, had Herzog been able to bury his mother after she died. Hired by Landrum as translator and guide, Herzog soon became head of the Overseas News Agency office in Vienna.

Herzog told Landrum that he knew who turned him in to the Nazis and vowed to find that man. He told Landrum, "I know he is alive. I haven't found him, but I know I will."

Years later it happened. As he reported to Landrum, "I was walking along the street in the heart of Vienna when I saw him. As he walked toward me, older and broken-looking, a voice inside me said, 'This hate has to stop somewhere; it might as well stop with you.' I passed him and I never looked back." Ralph and Nellie admired Herzog and repeated his story many times.

Ralph enjoyed working with Landrum on many projects, particularly activities for the benefit of Earlham, but their landmark efforts took place during the summer of 1962.

In 1934 Eli Lilly, always intensely interested in history, had purchased the estate of William Conner, one of Indiana's earliest pioneers. Conner and his brother John established a fur-trading network in Indiana. Each married a Delaware Indian woman and fathered children. When the Treaty of 1818 required the Delawares to move west, William Conner's Indian wife and children moved with them. He remained in Indiana, married a white woman, and built the estate near the present-day Noblesville, which Mr. Lilly bought.

With the best advice available in the 1930s, Mr. Lilly personally restored the historically significant house which sat on eighty acres of woods and prairie on the banks of the White River. Then, as he traveled around Indiana, he found a few abandoned log cabins, which he moved to the Conner property, thus creating a small pioneer village.

Now Mr. Lilly, wishing to preserve all this history and share it with the public, was looking for a new custodian for the property. He wished to give Conner Prairie to Earlham.

Landrum had a vision for developing the property. He proposed turning the Conner house and pioneer village into a living history museum. Then, using the land nearby, which formed a natural amphitheater, the facility could offer dramatic performances portraying the lives of the Delaware Indians and the Conners in the early days of the state. This idea excited not only Mr. Lilly but also Ralph Teetor. Long-time acquaintances, both of these men liked to indulge their nostalgia for pioneer times even while enjoying the last word in technological innovations. Over the course of the summer of 1962, Ralph, Landrum, and Eli Lilly crossed Lake Wawasee by boat many times as the Lilly and Teetor summer homes became the theater for working out a plan for Earlham to take possession of the Conner estate. As Mr. Lilly watched the museum grow under Earlham's leadership, he was simply delighted. In fact he was quoted as saying, "No other philanthropy has given me as much pure pleasure as Conner Prairie. I never dreamed it could become what it is."

Summers for the Teetor clan were still centering around the boats and cottages at Wawasee, but by the sixties one generation had dropped away and another come of age. Ralph and Nellie were now grandparents of four children and had moved to the smaller cottage, which Ralph rebuilt, leaving John, our children, and me the house in which I had grown up. Being in the house next door, I could appreciate how patient and gentle my father was. He loved having the grandchildren around and they were welcome at all hours. The children and their grandfather devised a marvelous game for rainy afternoons called "shoe store." The children pretended to sell him a new pair of shoes by trying to fit him in Nellie's size six, their own sneakers, and any other shoes they could find. Finally, of course, they fit his own shoes back on his feet which he declared to be "just perfect—exactly what I wanted." They would drag this out for an hour or more, knowing that in the end he would "buy" two or three pairs of his own shoes for a dime apiece. Was this a lesson in free enterprise?

During the summer of 1958, the radio news which Ralph always listened to was again reporting union threats in bargaining with the "Big Three" automobile manufacturers. Chrysler, General Motors, and Ford had agreed to a union shop many years before and had been forced to grant large wage increases during past bargaining rounds. After the strike at Perfect Circle in 1955, Ralph was concerned that concessions by the automotive giants would continue to intensify the pressure on the smaller companies. So he wrote to the presidents of the Big Three.

First he restated his strong opposition to forcing workers to join labor unions. Then he addressed what would become in twenty years the nemesis of the entire automobile industry—the loss of American market share because of labor costs which had been allowed to grow exorbitantly:

*. . . The other issue with which I am concerned is economic.*

*There is no one in industry who has any stronger desire than I to pay the highest wages and provide the best benefits possible in keeping with good business practice and sound economic principles. However, when we appraise today's market we can have only one position—that of holding the line against anything that would increase costs. To do otherwise would undoubtedly result in pricing ourselves out of more markets and adding to the inflationary spiral.*

*Because of our friendship and belief in the same principles, I am writing this to you.*

> *Most sincerely yours,*
> *Ralph R. Teetor*

By this time the Society of Automotive Engineers had grown into an international organization with Canadian, European, and Central and South American representation. That year Mr. Toyota, the president, and Mr. Yoshiki, the vice president of the newly-formed SAE of Japan, attended for the first time the international SAE annual convention at the Greenbriar in West Virginia. While they were in the United States, they visited several companies in the automotive industry, including Perfect Circle in Hagerstown. They were treated as honored guests everywhere, with Americans scrambling to learn the rudiments of Japanese protocol for giving gifts and preparing food to avoid insulting their distinguished guests.

Ralph and Nellie gave an elaborate dinner party in their home for the Japanese businessmen. Nellie, an accomplished hostess, fussed over the menu more than ever before, finally deciding on "elegant American" roast Cornish game hens, with appropriate accompaniments, and meringues for desert.

The next year American SAE visited Japan. John Warner, still General Manager of SAE and a close friend of Ralph's since 1936, John's wife Marion, Ralph, and Nellie carefully planned their tour of Japan. They expected to visit their new SAE friends, but they purposely included free time at every stop to keep the trip restful and pursue individual interests. Unknown to the Warners and Teetors, the Japanese had obtained a copy of their itinerary and filled every minute of leisure time with visits, parties, and receptions. When the Americans arrived at about two in the morning in Tokyo, they were met by Mr. Yoshiki, Mr. Ito, director of the Riken Piston Ring Company, and several members of the press. The next day their pictures were in all the papers, looking fresher and more alert than they felt. Having been treated as visiting celebrities, they affirmed that treatment accorded "the rich and famous" was not a way of living they would choose.

The exchange visits of the American and Japanese automotive engineers undoubtedly assisted the Japanese thrust into the international automobile markets. However, their success was probably as much the result of the decline of quality and efficiency in American companies and a favorable dollar-yen exchange rate as it was the quality of Japanese products. Had the U.S. companies remained alert and competitive, the Japanese would have had a more difficult task selling Hondas and Toyotas in this country a decade later.

Mr. Yoshiki did take information on the Speedostat back to Japan. Two years later Yoshiki returned to Detroit. This time the red carpet was not unrolled. Just prior to his arrival, Perfect Circle received the following letter:

*Dear Sir:*

*Re: SPEEDOSTAT*

*We had recently a talking with a director of Technical Controlling Dept. of Toyota Motor Car Co. about the possibility of marketing your Speedostat for Japanese cars and the following are the resume of their opinion.*

*1. At the present stage, the instrument may be sold to some limited car owners in Japan but not demanded by majority, because there are not many freeways in Japan yet where allow the drivers run utilizing fully the Speedostat.*

*2. Tokico, a motor car parts maker, are nearly completed the similar device to yours.*

*3. They say, they hear, in some district in USA the use of the Speedostat is prohibited for the reason that it is rather dangerous relaxing drivers to over extent, sometimes sleeping.*

*4. The technique of manufacturing the instrument is rather easy for Japanese factories and if your instrument is not protected by patent they need not your assistance or know-how.*

*5. Japanese makers can probably manufacture the Speedostat at lower cost in Japan and, if you desire, they shall be able to supply you the product of your design from here which will be more profitable to you.*

*Mr. Yoshiki will arrive at Detroit on Oct. 24 and leave there on 26. He says, he wish to meet some of you during his stay in Detroit.*

The only reply from Perfect Circle was a terse assurance that there were no areas in the United States that prohibited the use of the Speedostat and that they would try to meet Mr. Yoshiki in Detroit. There is no record of who met with him but it definitely was not Ralph.

It took several years for the Speedostat to become profitable for Perfect Circle. While it became more popular each year, successful marketing of a new product required a great deal of sales effort. New-car dealers had to be persuaded to demonstrate the Stat's advantages. Automotive service departments had to be trained to install and service this new mechanical device. And Perfect Circle needed to convince the public that Speedostat was a desirable car option.

It was the gasoline crisis of 1972–73 that finally made the Stat a fully accepted accessory. By this time the device had been significantly changed. Forgotten was the dashboard dial that could be preset to a desired speed; also gone was the resistance under the accelerator. To reduce its cost, the Stat was now simply an automatic throttle holding at whatever speed the car was traveling when the driver connected it. And the name by which it was known in most every showroom was "Cruise Control."

Some time in the early 1960s, Ralph Edwards of the then popular television show "This Is Your Life" contacted Nellie to solicit her assistance in producing a show about Ralph Teetor. With Dad on camera, the show planned to bring in his friends and associates, childhood to current, while Edwards narrated his life and accomplishments. Dad was to have no prior knowledge of the proposed show, because it was supposed to be a complete surprise. But Mother had a problem: Dad hated surprises of that type. She and I agreed that he had to be told. His reply was a flat, uncompromising "NO!" I don't think he ever told anyone and it wasn't mentioned again.

For many years the directors of Perfect Circle had been concerned with the future management of the company. If the business was to remain in the family, the next generation needed to be trained. It was during the late 1940s that the first members of the third generation of Teetors began to examine the possibilities of an inherited career. But the world had changed. There were too many of us. The only fair policy, company directors decided, was to prohibit all of us from counting on a career at Perfect Circle. And so it was.

That didn't solve the problem of the future leadership of the company. In 1950 Perfect Circle planned a merger with Thompson Products, a firm manufacturing other automotive parts. However, Thompson Products owned a small piston ring division which made a very limited type of ring. On the final day before the merger was to be completed, the federal government denied the merger, fearing that the combination of the two piston ring companies could be a monopoly. Ralph, considering their worries overblown, was disgusted and disappointed.

Several years later, as Ralph was again spending time with his friends in Detroit selling the Stat, he attempted to generate interest in a merger with General Motors. The rest of his colleagues lacked enthusiasm. More years passed, and by 1960 most of Perfect Circle's management was looking forward to retirement. Everyone now recognized that something needed to be done.

In 1960 Perfect Circle opened a manufacturing plant in Mexico. Coincidentally, Dana Corporation, which specialized in supplying parts to the trucking industry, was preparing to manufacture there as well. As Bill Prosser made many trips to Mexico for Perfect Circle, he became acquainted with the managers of Dana, flying in the same plane as they did and discussing many of the concerns shared by both automotive companies. As the men from the two companies became better acquainted, they found a rich compatibility between their organizations, even though Dana was about four times larger than Perfect Circle. From that beginning came the agreement to merge the companies. In 1963 Perfect Circle became a wholly-owned subsidiary of Dana Corporation. All of the Teetors still in management promptly retired. Included in all the announcements to the community and to the employees was Dana's assurance that "nothing would change." Naturally, nothing could have been further from the truth.

During the negotiations Ralph, of course, became acquainted with the members of management. From them, Ralph received ample assurance that the Speedostat project would continue to be a high priority with Dana, so he had no difficulty agreeing to retire. After all, he was seventy-three years old and he could get along very well without the salary. He even believed that he would be invited to be a member of the Dana board of directors. It never occurred to him that he would be expected to relinquish his office at the factory and his informal position as director of Speedostat engineering. Shortly after the merger, Dana requested that he move out entirely. The Dana board position was given to his cousin, Donald. Ralph was bitterly disappointed. Suddenly he was cut off from the day-to-day life of the company he had loved since he was five years old. It was a very difficult adjustment.

As time went on he worried about the employees, too. Gradually, they were made aware that a new culture prevailed at Perfect Circle; management was more impersonal now. The company wasn't so interested in the little community of Hagerstown. It wasn't going to support every activity in the town that requested money or help as Perfect Circle had done. Many of the Teetors' younger friends were required to move to Toledo, Dana's headquarters. Layoffs were more frequent and lasted longer; some became permanent. Then one by one Dana closed many factories in the Perfect Circle system. As the automotive industry in the United States faced the foreign competition of which Ralph had warned, threatened first by European imports and then by the Japanese, some Perfect Circle operations were moved to more advantageous locations. Other operations were merged into existing Dana manufacturing centers. The buzzwords became "lean and mean" for survival.

Perfect Circle employees reacted with disappointment and low morale. Profits plunged. Dana management thought that they had been deceived into buying a "hick" company. Although Dana had pledged to maintain the Perfect Circle name, top management now ordered the name eliminated.

Some wiser Dana employees objected, suggesting that they run a market survey on name recognition and its relationship to reputation. The survey showed that Perfect Circle was the most respected name for piston rings. Dana was then best known for—perfume! The Perfect Circle name was restored.

It is interesting to speculate what might have happened to Perfect Circle had it not been sold to Dana or anyone else. Looking back from the vantage point of thirty-two years later it appears that consolidation could not have been avoided for long. The world changed so much in the thirty years following this decision that Perfect Circle might also have been forced, like Dana, to make difficult and unpopular decisions to survive amid the intensifying competition. It was not a time when a company could afford to be humane and gentle. Perfect Circle had read the future many times and had responded to change well, but there were no easy alternatives in a world of tightening competition and acquisition ethics. Although no one in Hagerstown would want to agree, folding the tents and selling may have been the best decision. But Ralph stated many times that had he known what it would be like, he would never have voted for the merger. Ten years later he told a visiting reporter, "Every morning when I wake up I think, 'I wish I hadn't sold Perfect Circle.'"

Ironically, the last Perfect Circle employee was "retired" and the last factory door in Hagerstown was closed exactly one hundred years after it all began.

*(Top) Mr. Yoshiki of SAE, Japan, and Ralph examine the Speedostat during Mr. Yoshiki's visit to Hagerstown, 1958.*

*(Bottom) Ralph visits with Rene McPherson, president of Dana Corporation, during his visit to Perfect Circle to celebrate the company's seventy-fifth anniversary in 1970.*

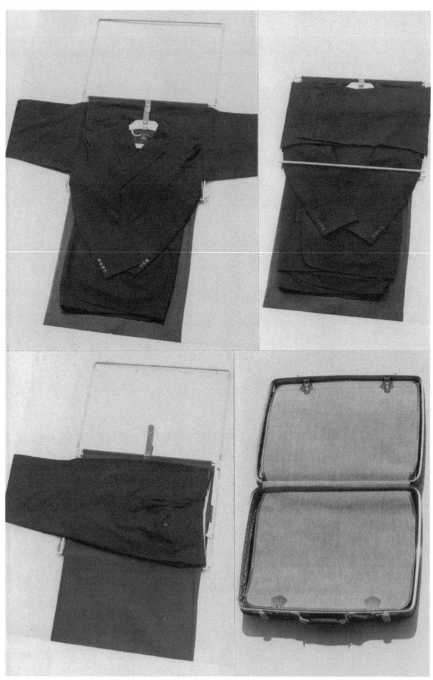

*Photos illustrated the suitfolder instructions.*

*Detailed suitfolder instructions were written by Ralph but most people found them too complicated to bother with.*

# Creative Factor Is Thought, Says Blind Inventor on Visit

## Head of Corporation Develops Many Devices

### By WALTER GOODSTEIN

A New Orleans visitor, qualified to make the observation, said Wednesday that "the only real creative factor is the ability to think: You don't create with your eyes."

He was Ralph Teetor, Hagerstown, Ind., engineer and inventor. Teetor has been blind since he was five years old.

President and active operator of the Perfect Circle Corporation, he has developed numerous engine devices used by the automobile and aviation industries.

A graduate of the University of Pennsylvania, 1912, Teetor demonstrated creative mechanical talents long before then. At the age of 12 he completed building an automobile by himself. This information was volunteered by his cousin, Macy O. Teetor of New Orleans.

### Plans 'Speedostat'

While he has concentrated on developing piston rings for engines, Teetor finds enjoyment also in inventing unusual products. He discussed a more recent one on Wednesday — a speedostat.

"This gadget is a driving aid to the motorist who wishes to maintain a constant speed," he said.

"To prevent the driver from overrunning a desired speed, whether it be 25 miles per hour or 80, this speedostat is adjusted under the accelerator pedal. It

—Photo by The Times-Picayune.
RALPH TEETOR

national council of Boy Scouts of America, and membership on the Society of Automotive Engineers, which he headed in 1936.

Teetor is married and has a daughter who is attending Northwestern university. She is studying science and chemistry.

Teetor plans to spend a week in New Orleans visiting relatives.

*Ralph listens to his minute repeater pocket watch.*

*Ralph loved his daughter's family — John Meyer, Lucy, Jennifer, Ralph, Ruth, and Marjorie, as seen here in 1960.*

# Walking the Red Carpets

Ralph carried the burden of selling Perfect Circle to Dana more than did the rest of the family. Many of the Teetors moved from Hagerstown as soon as the merger was completed. Lothair had died in 1961; Macy had already retired and moved to New Orleans. Don and Herman Teetor and Bill Prosser left town for warmer climates. Dan Teetor and Blair Hartley, both in their late seventies, were ready to retire but kept their residences in Hagerstown.

Mourning what might have been was not, of course, something Ralph was going to allow himself to do. He had too much to accomplish. He still attended SAE meetings with his friends and kept up on all the news of the automobile industry. One friend asked him if he was going to quit working now that he was retired. He answered, "Oh, no, I'm thinking of starting another company!"

When the Corvair was introduced in the fall of 1959, Ed Cole took Ralph on a ride during one of his Detroit visits. The car had a rear engine design and represented General Motors' first venture into the small car market. Ralph never really liked small cars, but he agreed that this one was better than he had expected. Most auto enthusiasts loved it. *Motor Trend* magazine proclaimed it "Car of the Year." When Ralph Nader's book *Unsafe at any Speed* was published in 1965, denouncing not only the Corvair but the entire automotive industry, Ralph was furious. He saw it as the beginning of a dangerous trend in determining responsibility by government regulation. It prompted the following letter:

*Mr. Ralph Nader*
*Dear Sir:*

*Since I am deeply interested in the automotive industry, I am writing you this letter to give you my comments on your book* Unsafe At Any Speed.

*By way of introduction, I was head of the engineering and President of Perfect Circle Corporation for more than fifty years. Since the Perfect Circle Corporation has for the past fifty-five years been a major supplier of piston rings to the principle automobile builders, I have worked very closely with many of the engineers in the industry and am well acquainted with their constant effort to build the maximum safety into their cars.*

*I also originated the Auto Pilot and Cruise Control which is designed to give the driver safety speed warning and control, and is now offered by many makes of automobiles.*

*With those qualifications I feel justified to tell you that because you have concentrated practically all of your condemnation for the cause of highway accidents on the design of automobiles, you have relieved the drivers of their responsibility for safe driving.*

*It is impossible to build a practical automobile that is safe when driven by an unreliable driver. Therefore, the only way to reduce highway accidents is to allow only better drivers to drive cars and to prohibit the irresponsible drivers from driving. We must pass laws containing severe punishment and make certain courts impose the prescribed punishment when the drivers are found in violation.*

*Your most detrimental and unfair statements concern the performance of the Society of Automotive Engineers. It has been my privilege to be an active member of the Society for fifty-four years, and during that time I have served on every administrative and technical committee, and as president. I know from personal experience that vehicle safety is a major concern of the SAE. The Society is the cooperative engineering clearing house of the greatest free enterprise industry this world has ever known. And instead of your claim to improve the safety of the automobile, you are introducing political elements that will be of no value, but will only serve to interfere with future progress.*

*I am keenly interested in doing anything that will reduce our traffic hazard. This is evidenced by my having been for many years a member of the Indiana Traffic Safety Council which is devoted entirely to traffic safety. Also, I am enclosing a copy of an article which appeared in the May 1965 issue of* Traffic Safety *magazine, and if you read it, you will understand the interest and concern I have expressed for many years.*

News of Ralph Nader turned the normally patient and tolerant Ralph Teetor's temper up to boil. Anyone within earshot would hear again just what evil Ralph Nader was promoting.

The Perfect Circle engineers who had been working with Ralph on the Speedostat had moved out of his building. Only Bob Morris remained behind to assist Ralph in his well-equipped workshop. Bob had always been employed by Ralph rather than Perfect Circle. With the Speedostat gone they turned their attention to the suitcase folder. They began to prepare it for possible production, testing different materials for the frame, finally settling on aluminum tubing. They bought an industrial sewing machine and a bolt of appropriately-heavy brown cloth for the cover. Bob learned to sew the covers to the fine tolerances that Ralph required, tolerances which had caused Nellie so much frustration. And of course Ralph applied for a patent, eventually obtaining a very good one.

Ralph always did all his own sourcing of supplies and tooling for all of his inventions and directed outside manufacturing of parts for both prototypes and future production. Now he was looking for hooks and snaps, hangers and swivels. The customer would not know how to use the wonderful new traveling suitfolder unless instructions accompanied this product, so Ralph wrote them. Then he called upon Perfect Circle photographer Don Beeson to photograph each step needed to pack a suit. Don marveled at the precise plan Ralph had devised. When he finished photographing, Don recalled that Ralph asked him, "Why did you use two different size flash bulbs?" Ralph felt the difference in the heat they emitted. He then examined Don's camera, running his hands over the outside and asking him about the lens and film speed. "When he was finished he told me more about how that camera worked than I had ever known," declared Don. "And his hands never once touched the lens."

It took different-sized suitfolders to fit each size of suitcase. Ralph called on luggage manufacturers to introduce his superior product, but it was harder to sell the folder without the reputation he had established in the automotive industry over almost sixty years. Selling the suitfolder was difficult, too, because there were several precise steps to packing it successfully, so the average person needed a demonstration to understand it. Nellie exclaimed that it took an engineer to use the device. While she knew she was exaggerating, her comment acknowledged that it required some patience to learn Ralph's system. Ralph, of course, was sure that the results were worth the small bit of extra effort. Several luggage companies including Johnson's Eagle and Skyway were interested at first and a number of leading luggage stores carried the folder for a short time. Eventually they gave up because of the difficulty and expense of training employees to give demonstrations. Finally, Ralph enjoyed giving the folders away to friends.

But he hadn't given up on the idea of one more company. Building, research, development, even selling, were just too much fun to turn his back on. One day he was overheard calling his stock broker. He asked many questions about the Schick Razor Company—number of shares outstanding, capitalization, annual sales, profitability. It was obvious that the broker was advising him not to purchase Schick stock. Ralph replied, "Oh, I wasn't planning to buy stock. I was thinking of buying the company!"

I doubt if he was thinking too seriously about that. Mother would have blown up at the suggestion.

Nellie was not sitting at home eating bonbons these days. Running a neat and orderly house and supporting Ralph in everything he did was unquestionably her first priority. She also looked after Ralph's mother, her mother, and a few elderly aunts as long as they lived. In 1952 she started volunteering as a gray lady at Reid Memorial Hospital in Richmond and continued to do that for twenty-three years. In 1962 she was elected to the hospital board of trustees, where she served eleven years before being appointed a life member. She had no problem switching from the role of top authority to the bottom of the ladder. She enjoyed both activities and was beloved by both groups of associates.

Ralph was very protective of his wife. Although she was a good driver, he didn't really like for her to drive long distances. The seventeen miles to Richmond was acceptable, but sixty miles to Indianapolis was stretching it. Nellie never complained other than to say, "Oh, Ralph, I'm sure I won't have any trouble."

But more and more as Ralph grew older he would reply, "I would just feel better if Horace drove you to Indianapolis. Could you go one day later?" And of course she would.

One day she was starting home from her gray lady job at the hospital, driving a brand-new Cadillac, when she had a fender-bender accident at the edge of town. Her new Cadillac was rumpled but drivable. She knew that if Ralph learned what had happened, he would curtail her independence even more. So instead of driving straight home, she drove back to the Cadillac dealership in Richmond where the new car had been purchased just a few days before. There she asked them for another car exactly like the one she was driving. They didn't have one but they found a duplicate in Dayton which they could have delivered and ready for her in about two hours. "That's fine, I'll wait here," she told them.

By the time Ralph came home for dinner that night she was there to greet him, calm and cheerful as always, having just purchased the only car she ever bought by herself. This lady, so thrifty that she darned Ralph's socks when they had a hole, never told anyone what had happened. It was probably the only event of any consequence that ever happened to her that she did not share with Ralph.

Creative people are usually curious about almost everything. While chatting informally with a Brazilian member at an SAE meeting in 1962 several of the engineers, including Ralph, became intrigued with the Brazilian babassu nut. This small, round, hard nut was about an inch and a quarter in diameter. Although known to be inedible, it was reputed to contain a kernel of valuable oil if only one could find an economical way of cracking it and extracting the soft meat inside. The project combined two of Ralph's favorite activities— inventing a better way of doing something and cracking nuts.

While Ralph enjoyed eating any kind of nuts, macadamia and black walnuts were his favorites. And half the fun was getting there. He considered himself to be an "expert" nutcracker. The mechanics of getting the nutmeat out of the shell in as unbroken a condition as possible presented a fascinating challenge to him. He had, over the years, made models of some of his best ideas for nutcrackers—screw types, pinchers, and cutters. For birthdays or Christmas his grandchildren gave him nutcrackers in every shape and size, each of which, as he received it, he invariably declared did the best job he had ever seen. In spite of all the clever mechanics, the method he preferred for the Christmas pecans and black walnuts was a steel plate he had built into the windowsill in the garage of his home. On this nutcracking platform, he tapped the nuts with a small hammer.

The babassu nut defied cracking. Nature had locked it up and dared man to find the key. With a potentially commercial reward, the challenge was enticing to Ralph, so he asked Alaric Paris, his Brazilian SAE friend, to send him some nuts. In a few weeks two sacks with over fifty pounds of babassu nuts were delivered to the door. Bob Morris related that he first tried to crack one of the nuts with a sledge hammer on the concrete floor, but "that sent it ricocheting about the room like a billiard ball." The only way he was able to open one was using a bandsaw with a metal-cutting blade. Bob added, "These things even had the mice neurotic. We would find the nuts with teeth marks on them but no mouse ever got through."

The little group of SAE engineers had fun sending each other tongue-in-cheek engineering reports, mechanical drawings, and theoretical proposals for extracting the kernels of the babassu nuts. Finally Ralph wrote to Reg Pigott, an engineering friend in Pittsburgh, "John Warner has just written me that you are interested in trying to crack some babassu nuts. I have a plentiful supply on hand and will send you some so that you may try your luck. I worked on a scheme for cracking the nuts, but it got so complicated I decided to let the Brazilians crack them any way they wanted to. The fact is, I had some other projects that were so much more interesting and which I thought would be more productive that I decided to give up the 'nut cracking suite.' "

Black walnuts, however, were a different matter. Another of the good Quaker friends of the family was kind, gentle Jim Cope. A biology professor at Earlham College in Richmond, Jim loves God's earth and all that grows on it. His students not only learned about that world but also developed a deep appreciation of the exquisiteness of creation. Although Jim's areas of specialty are birds and bats, it was his knowledge of trees that drew Ralph and Jim together on this special project in 1968. Jim had been studying the variety of soils in eastern Indiana left by the action of four different glaciers which crossed that area at different periods of history. He learned that, as a result of one of these glaciers, Wayne County grew the best black walnut trees in the world. That caught Ralph's attention, especially when he ascertained that his property included some of this wonderful Wisconsin Glaciation soil. Besides, the story of Johnny Appleseed had always intrigued Ralph. A couple of gnarly old apple trees in his Wawasee yard were credited, no doubt with wishful thinking, to the planting of Johnny Appleseed. Ralph eventually planted black walnut trees—hundreds of them—over forty acres. After obtaining all the trees that were in the tree nurseries in the area, he resorted to trees from the State of Indiana as one year old seedlings. Purdue was working on a project to improve varieties of nut trees by grafting, but Ralph didn't want any part of that. "No, that seems a bit like cheating," he told Jim.

"What do you mean, it is cheating?" Jim asked him.

"Well, I just think we ought to let nature decide these things," Ralph answered. Jim tried to explain that, due to cross pollination, planting a walnut seed did not guarantee that the same kind of walnut tree would grow from the seed that it had produced. Only by grafting could one assure the species of the new tree. Ralph was unconvinced, so Jim gathered walnuts from the desired varieties and propagated them at the Hays Arboretum for a year or more before planting them in Ralph's walnut groves.

In addition to many different varieties of black walnut, they put in some pecan trees too. Ralph paid close attention to how the trees were planted, walking down to the area frequently to see how they were taking hold and then reporting to Jim.

That same year Ralph was seventy-eight years old. He knew that the trees would not produce a crop of nuts for at least twenty years, so he would not gather the fruit. But to him, planting black walnut trees was an excellent way to leave the world a little better than he found it.


Ralph believed that a carefully thought-out gift to education was also an investment in a better future. He didn't seek personal recognition and usually discouraged the use of his name. The gift he made to SAE in 1963 to establish the Ralph R. Teetor SAE Education Fund combined his commitment to education and his lifelong devotion to engineering. The Teetor Fund each year sends young engineers to the SAE meetings and conventions to see for themselves the value of the interchange of technical information and collaboration with the collected wisdom of the participants. In his last years he made a point of meeting personally with each new group of recipients. Ralph also allowed his name to be placed on a planetarium which he donated to Earlham. Again he was solving visual problems for sighted people.

Although Ralph had always received ample recognition for the things he was doing, his retirement signaled an even greater outpouring of honors and celebrations of his accomplishments. Nineteen-sixty-five brought two honorary degrees, Doctor of Engineering at the Indiana Institute of Technology at Fort Wayne, Indiana, and Doctor of Laws at Earlham College. That same spring he was made a Fellow in the American Society of Mechanical Engineers. Mother said she was watching him carefully that his head didn't grow too big.

August 17, 1970, Ralph celebrated his eightieth birthday at Lake Wawasee. He discouraged the idea of a party, so his friends around the world sent him audio tapes of greetings and reminiscences. The children gave him his traditional macadamia nuts and coconut birthday cake and probably another nutcracker. He enjoyed himself immensely but a fire seemed to go out that day. Not a word was said, but I'm sure he realized that he had finally reached a goal. He had proven that he could do whatever he wanted to do and he could do it well, living a normal and happy eighty years, achieving almost everything he had set out to do. Now he could relax.

There were no more plans to start another business. A new idea didn't send him immediately to the basement to tinker. Arthritis in his hips made walking a chore, which also contributed to his decision to slow down a bit. However, none of this discouraged his friends and the institutions he had served: the celebrations of his achievements continued.

The Indiana Academy was formed by the presidents of the seventeen colleges which made up the Associated Colleges of Indiana, the college and industry fund raising partnership which Ralph, Frank Sparks, and Tom Jones had established nearly twenty years before. The Academy was established to "honor persons, both living and deceased, who have made significant contributions to the state through public service, higher education, arts, sciences, literature, and general culture." In October, 1971, they chose Ralph Teetor to be a member of their first group of twenty-five living honorees.

Two years later SAE built a new national headquarters in Warrendale, Pennsylvania. The lane leading to the new building was named Ralph R. Teetor Lane.

The Masonic Lodge Ralph had joined so many years before was a popular organization in Hagerstown, and many of Ralph's friends belonged. In the early 1970s the Hagerstown lodge needed a new headquarters. Ralph owned a lot in town at the top of a hill with a lovely view of the sweeping Indiana farmland behind it. (This one he had been saving for me if I ever moved back to Hagerstown.) Assured that I would not need it, he offered it to the Masons for a new lodge and assisted their fund-raising for the building.

For some time Ralph's Masonic friends had believed Ralph should be awarded the 33d degree, an honorary award for contribution to Masons and the community. No one from Hagerstown had ever received this honor and it would be a thrill for the lodge, too, if Ralph were selected. The new building, however, became an obstacle to a few people who saw it as a means of "buying" his way into the 33d. Ralph's friends, insisting that nothing could have been further from the truth, persisted.

The following spring Ralph was chosen to receive the "Good Friend and Neighbor" award at the annual banquet cosponsored by the Hagerstown Rotary Club and a committee of farmers. Don McCullough, Rotarian, Mason, and always a jovial master of ceremonies, was in charge of the program. This consisted of a "This is Your Life" review of Ralph's life with significant people greeting him at appropriate moments—all supposedly a surprise to Ralph. After the Ralph Edwards affair, Nellie had warned him of this one too, but he loved his hometown and agreed to let it happen, even enjoying the result—all the while swearing that he was totally surprised. Don was also spearheading the 33d degree promotion, and he surmised that, properly planned, this program might further that cause. It appears to have been a good strategy, because early in 1976, Ralph was notified that he had been elected to receive the Scottish Rite 33d degree.

For many years men had traveled to Scotland to receive this honor, but in more recent times it has been conferred once a year in Boston. With arthritis progressively debilitating him, Ralph informed Don that he could not go to Boston. Then Don discovered that there would be a ceremony in Minneapolis and offered to take Ralph there in an ambulance but that too was rejected. Don reported that Nellie's exact words were, "He isn't even going to Modoc," (a village about six miles from Hagerstown). Don didn't give up.

Ralph Teetor received the 33d degree at Hagerstown Lodge 49 on May 12, 1976. Seventy-five men came in by bus from Indianapolis to conduct the ceremony. I don't know if the 33d degree of the Masonic order was ever before conferred to one individual in a special ceremony in his hometown, but it was done in Hagerstown for Ralph.

Dana Corporation also joined in celebrating Ralph's lifetime career achievement. The new Perfect Circle Ralph R. Teetor Engineering and Test Center was built in Richmond in 1977. At the October first dedication Ben Basile, Perfect Circle Division President, told the one hundred people present:

*This test center has the latest modern equipment available to meet our needs in testing our products to ensure leadership in the future. It is fitting that we dedicate such a facility to a gentleman who has always looked to the future.*

It was 1980, SAE's seventy-fifth anniversary, and a gala event was being planned in Detroit. Ralph was ninety. Not only did he receive the official invitations and information, but the past recipients of his scholarship award especially urged him to come. Ralph sent his regrets, saying his arthritis made travel too difficult. His assistant JoAnne Warmoth, who had read the correspondence to him, said, "Oh, Mr. Teetor, if you go to Detroit, they are going to have a red carpet out for you from the time you step off of that plane until the time you leave."

Ralph smiled at her and slowly replied, "JoAnne, I've celebrated all my red carpets."

Ralph Teetor's life spanned the entire development of the automobile industry in the United States and he participated in much of the technology which made that field successful. As he and his engineering friends collaborated, they consciously realized that they were traveling on a course that would revolutionize American cultural patterns. They greeted each new day with anticipation, because it always led either to a better solution or a new direction. Through the technical jargon in the engineers' letters and reports one can sense the vision these pioneers saw of a new world of opportunities, comforts, and safety. Perhaps Ralph said it best to the president of Young Radiator Company, Fred Young, one of his fellow engineers in solving America's transportation problems, when Young wrote to tell him of some new technology:

*I really would have enjoyed the visit with you at the DeLaval plant at Trenton, for that was one of the shop visits that I made during my senior year at the University of Pennsylvania in 1912. At that time one of their popular products was the steam-driven cream separator. Time goes on, and we cannot predict what technological progress will produce during the next generation. However, I am sure it will not be any more colorful and interesting than the period in which you and I are living.*

Was Ralph handicapped? Jack Swoveland, another of the Speedostat engineers, talked with him after his retirement. He asked Ralph, "With all that you have been able to accomplish, what more do you think you would have done if you had been able to see?"

Ralph replied, "I probably couldn't have done as much, because I can concentrate and you can't."

When Jack asked Ralph what he thought he had received from all his work on the Speedostat, Ralph answered, "Look at all the lives it has touched, the jobs it has provided, not only at Perfect Circle, but suppliers, mechanics, and others, and the pleasure and added safety it has brought to so many drivers. That gives me a lot of satisfaction."

That satisfaction was lifelong. Ralph Teetor died on February 15, 1982, after a short illness, and Nellie followed him on October 8, 1984.

In high school I played the part of Emily in Thorton Wilder's *Our Town*. Toward the end of the play, after Emily has died and is watching her friends mourn her death, another deceased character declares, "That's all human beings are! Just blind people." Emily's response is, "They don't understand, do they? They're sort of shut up in little boxes, aren't they?"

Ralph Teetor's vision and determination enabled him to see beyond his boxes. He insisted that he was not unique, that just about anyone, with concentration and practice, could do the same.

Perhaps he was right.

Ralph received the 33d degree of the Masonic Lodge in 1976. Seated (left to right): W. Henry Roberts, 33d degree; Nellie Teetor, Ralph Teetor, Marjorie Teetor Meyer, F. A. Wakeman, 33d degree. Standing: John Meyer, Ruth Meyer, Robert L. Miller, 33d degree; Jennifer Meyer, Lucinda Meyer, C. Kyle Hughes, 33d degree.

Dana Corporation honored Ralph by naming Dana's new engineering test center the Ralph R. Teetor Test Center in 1977. Pictured at the dedication ceremony were Marjorie, Ralph, Ben Basile, Vice President of Dana and General Manager of Perfect Circle Division, and Nellie.

In 1974 SAE named a road leading to its international headquarters in Warrendale, Pennsylvania, Ralph Teetor Lane. Past presidents of SAE representing Ralph at the ceremony were John C Ellis of Shell Oil Corporation, Eugene J. Manganiello of NASA, Wilson A Gebhardt of Bendix Corporation, and Arch T. Calwell of Thompson Products, later TRW Corporation.

*Ralph R. Teetor was inducted into the Automotive Hall of Fame in Midland, Michigan, in 1988.*

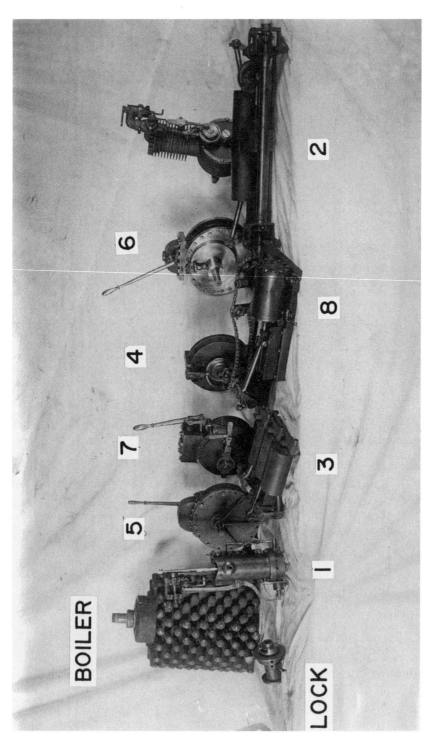

*Charles Teetor's early experimental engines.*

# Appendix

In 1895, after Charles Teetor invented the railway inspection car which was powered like a bicycle, he worked four years to create a lightweight engine powerful enough to propel the car. The automotive industry was still quite primitive and no satisfactory machines for such use yet existed. So the engines pictured here represent very early pioneering in the industry, and the many failures were due to the lack of knowledge of many of the fundamental characteristics which are required to make a successful engine. Each of these was designed and handmade solely by Charles N. Teetor, and are displayed at the Hagerstown Museum in Hagerstown, Indiana. They are numbered in the order in which they were made.

Numbers one and two, made in 1895 and 1896 respectively, were internal combustion engines. The first vibrated excessively and shook the car to pieces while both overheated due to lack of cooling fins. By 1897 there was considerable effort to produce a successful steam-propelled automobile, so over the next three years, Charles made six different small steam engines, none of which was satisfactory, They are numbered three through eight.

After these engines were built and tested, a successful single-cylinder gasoline engine was produced and built into a small railway car. It satisfactorily transported three passengers on the railroad and yet was not too heavy to be removed from the track by one man to allow trains to pass. Production began in 1901.

The engine on the right of the back row is a single-cylinder, three-horsepower stationary engine that was manufactured in 1905 by the Light Inspection Car Company. Several hundred of these were made and sold during the first decade of the twentieth century. In 1909 that division of the company was sold to the Standard Pattern Manufacturing Company of Richmond, Indiana, who continued to make these engines for several years.

At the front, left side of the picture is the lock, designed and built by Zachariah Teeter, Charles Teetor, and Daniel Deardorff in 1895. During this period of America's history, train robberies were very common. Working in a railroad mail car, Daniel Deardorff conceived the idea of making a safe that could not be opened quickly after the train stopped. This lock has a cylinder and plunger which is supposed to be hooked to the air lines of the braking system of the train. When robbers stopped the train, the air pressure of the brakes also locked the safe which could not be opened until all the air was bled from the train. The time that it took to bleed the train was intended to give sufficient time for help to arrive to apprehend the robbers.

# Index

Marjorie Teetor Meyer attended Northwestern University and is a graduate of Butler University. She has served in leadership roles on a number of Hoosier philanthropic, educational and governmental boards of trustees, including Conner Prairie and Hanover College. Mrs. Meyer was named a Sagamore of the Wabash by the Governor of Indiana in 1984 and 1994. She has lived in Indianapolis more than forty years and is married to John R. Meyer. The couple has four children and five grandchildren.

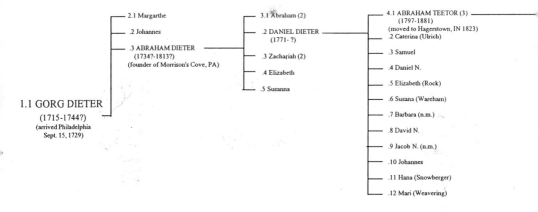

1.1 GORG DIETER

(1715-1744?)

(arrived Philadelphia
Sept. 15, 1729)

2.1 Margarthe

.2 Johannes

.3 ABRAHAM DIETER
(1734?-1813?)
(founder of Morrison's Cove, PA)

3.1 Abraham (2)

.2 DANIEL DIETER
(1771- ?)

.3 Zachariah (2)

.4 Elizabeth

.5 Susanna

4.1 ABRAHAM TEETOR (3)
(1797-1881)
(moved to Hagerstown, IN 1823)

.2 Caterina (Ulrich)

.3 Samuel

.4 Daniel N.

.5 Elizabeth (Rock)

.6 Susana (Wareham)

.7 Barbara (n.m.)

.8 David N.

.9 Jacob N. (n.m.)

.10 Johannes

.11 Hana (Snowberger)

.12 Mari (Weavering)

# THE TEETOR FAMILY TREE
## 1720 to 1930

This listing includes all known members of the Teetor Clan through the eighth generation in America. For this I am indebted to Charles J. Teetor, who has spent much time and effort on family research and generously allowed me to reprint these two pages from his book, *Charley Teetor's Hometown*.

*Codes: (nm) never married, (di) died infant*